case studies in
ARCHAEOLOGY

SERIES EDITOR
Jeffrey Quilter
Ripon College

PURISIMEÑO
CHUMASH PREHISTORY

MARITIME ADAPTATIONS
ALONG THE SOUTHERN CALIFORNIA COAST

PURISIMEÑO CHUMASH PREHISTORY

MARITIME ADAPTATIONS
ALONG THE SOUTHERN CALIFORNIA COAST

MICHAEL A. GLASSOW

Department of Anthropology
University of California, Santa Barbara

HARCOURT BRACE COLLEGE PUBLISHERS

FORT WORTH PHILADELPHIA SAN DIEGO NEW YORK ORLANDO AUSTIN SAN ANTONIO
TORONTO MONTREAL LONDON SYDNEY TOKYO

Publisher	TED BUCHHOLZ
Editor-in-Chief	CHRISTOPHER P. KLEIN
Senior Acquisitions Editor	STEPHEN T. JORDAN
Developmental Editor	MARGARET MCANDREW BEASLEY
Project Editor	JULIET GEORGE
Production Manager	DIANE GRAY
Art Director	MELINDA WELCH

Cover Image: Block Excavation near the beginning of excavations, Vandenberg Air Force Base. Photograph courtesy of Michael A. Glassow.

ISBN: 0-15-503084-1

Library of Congress Catalog Card Number: 95-80318

Address for Editorial Correspondence:
Harcourt Brace College Publishers, 301 Commerce Street, Suite 3700, Fort Worth, TX 76102.

Address for Orders:
Harcourt Brace & Company, 6277 Sea Harbor Drive, Orlando, FL 32887-6777.
1-800-782-4479, or 1-800-433-0001 (in Florida).

Printed in the United States of America

5 6 7 8 9 0 1 2 3 4   066   10 9 8 7 6 5 4 3 2 1

FOREWORD

ABOUT THE SERIES

These case studies in archaeology are designed to bring students, in beginning and intermediate courses in archaeology, anthropology, history, and related disciplines, insights into the theory, practice, and results of archaeological investigations. They are written by scholars who have had direct experience in archaeological research, whether in the field, laboratory, or library. The authors are also teachers, and in writing their books they have kept the students who will read them foremost in their minds. These books are intended to present a wide range of archaeological topics as case studies in a form and manner that will be more accessible than writings found in articles or books intended for professional audiences, yet at the same time preserve and present the significance of archaeological investigations for all.

ABOUT THE AUTHOR

Michael Glassow received his Ph.D. from UCLA in 1972, and he has been on the faculty at the University of California, Santa Barbara (UCSB), since 1969. Although the Santa Barbara Channel and adjacent regions have been the focus of his interest since his undergraduate days at UCLA, his earliest archaeological experiences were in the American Southwest, and his dissertation concerned the early development of prehistoric agricultural subsistence in northeastern New Mexico. His dissertation research was the beginning of his theoretical interest in the relationship between population growth and subsistence change, which is also reflected in this case study.

In addition to field research in California and the American Southwest, Glassow has worked in Jalisco, Mexico, and on occasion he lends a helping hand to his wife, Anabel Ford, an archaeologist studying the ancient Maya of Guatemala and Belize.

At UCSB Glassow teaches courses in traditional cultures of North America, California archaeology, and archaeological field and laboratory techniques. He is also curator of the Department of Anthropology's Repository for Archaeological and Ethnographic Collections and coordinator of the Central Coast Information Center, which houses the state's official cultural resource records and archives pertaining to Santa Barbara and San Luis Obispo Counties.

ABOUT THIS CASE STUDY

This case study holds a special place in my heart and mind because I was involved in some of the work that is discussed in it. In 1973, I packed my bags in Chicago and set out for the University of California, Santa Barbara. In those halcyon days of yore, when beads and long hair were still in fashion and Watergate was just entering the news, the prospect of spending some time on the West Coast was not an unreasonable consideration in deciding where to go to graduate school, at least for me.

Within a short time after I arrived, I became actively involved in local archaeology, along with fellow graduate students. We were encouraged to do so by UCSB faculty to both hone our archaeological skills and to take advantage of the income provided by salvage work, a consequence of a regional building-boom.

After my initial experiences in the field and lab, I had a number of strong impressions of archaeology in California. I was charmed by the beauty of the landscape—the magnificent stretches of coast, the fairy-like oak glades of the foothills, and the majestic expanses of interior mountain wilderness. The prehistory was much more interesting than I had imagined it to be. Californian Native Americans were the authors of complex social systems, elaborate exchange networks, and rich religious traditions.

At the same time, however, I was appalled by the provincial attitudes held by many specialists in the archaeology of the state, especially some of my graduate school peers. They seemed to know or care very little about anything other than California archaeology. Was there some ancient continuum of traditional provincialism? Californian Native American cultures manifested one of the greatest diversities in languages in North America (due likely to isolation). In contemporary California, all land east of the Sierra Nevada Mountains was referred to as Out East. The narrow world view of the archaeologists seemed to partake of the same lack of interest. In many senses, the prehistory of California was and is a world onto itself.

But I was lucky enough to be under the tutelage of Dr. Michael A. Glassow. He was able to demonstrate that while the archaeology of the region could be appreciated in its own right, it also was of great importance as a field in which a number of important questions about past human behavior could be investigated. Issues concerning the way humans interact with each other and with coastal resources and changes in them through time were available for study. Approaching Californian archaeology in this way proved invaluable to me in my study of the archaeology of coastal Peru.

I therefore recommend this case study to the reader as both an opportunity to learn about the prehistory of one area of the coast of California and about how some of the essential questions regarding human-environmental relations and their changes have been studied there. The details of excavation, the changing research questions as new data are revealed, and the difficulties of working in the context of "salvage" archaeology are put forth in clear prose. This book will serve a wide variety of purposes to instruct students in many topics as well as to help provide greater recognition and appreciation for the rich archaeological heritage of California.

JEFFREY QUILTER
Series Editor
Ripon, Wisconsin

PREFACE

Today southern California coastal environments are popular for their picturesque sunsets, sunny sands, and rhythmic sounds of crashing surf. The prehistoric inhabitants of the southern California coast probably also appreciated these aspects of the coastal environment, but more than likely they were much more interested in the coastal environment as a provider of a wide variety of food products and materials for making artifacts. Indeed, we may presume that they frequently lived just above a beach not for the spectacular views but instead for easy access to these resources. Marine resources still are of considerable importance to those of us who live along or near the southern California coast, of course, even though our land-oriented daily lives insulate most of us from intimate contact with the coastal environment.

Despite the attractions of marine resources, prehistoric inhabitants of the southern California coast confronted a number of challenges in acquiring them due in large part to being mammals adapted to living on land rather than in the sea. Aboriginal coast-dwellers met these challenges by employing two basic resource acquisition strategies. One of these was to take advantage of opportune circumstances of access when they occurred. For example, coast-dwellers waited for low tides to expose the most productive beds of mussels and other shellfish, or they routinely checked coastal rocks to see whether seals or sea lions were hauled out. The second strategy was to use sophisticated capture technology such as nets, hook-and-line, and harpoons. Because both strategies were associated with costs in time and effort, southern California marine resources were not always as attractive as their abundance might imply, and it should not be surprising, therefore, that terrestrial resources remained important throughout at least 9,000 years of southern California prehistory.

Yet marine resources also were utilized throughout all this prehistory. In fact, they became as important as terrestrial resources to the prehistoric ancestors of the Purisimeño Chumash people by at least 8,000 years ago. As this case study reveals, the story of how and why marine resources were utilized by the Purisimeño Chumash and their predecessors is a complicated one, made so by continual changes through the course of prehistory in the marine and terrestrial environments, the artifacts used to acquire and process marine resources, and social and economic institutions. Because the prehistory of the Purisimeño Chumash extends back 9,000 years, and because their habitation sites dating after 8,500 years ago are rich in the bones and shells from marine animals they hunted or collected, research into how and why marine resources became important has a good chance of producing fruitful results. I attempted to take advantage of these potentials in the research reported in this case study. In particular, I document in the following chapters the major aspects of the evolution of a coastal way of life, and I propose possible explanations for this evolution, which of course did not simply "happen."

Why bother to elucidate the evolution of a maritime culture and search for explanations of its evolutionary trajectory? The self-centered answer to this question is that I find these endeavors intellectually challenging, and I derive a lot of enjoyment from the field and laboratory work and the data analysis. In the course of my research, for example, I have had to learn much about such fields as marine biology, geochemistry, and climate, and I have begun to collaborate with natural scientists who are experts in different aspects of marine environment. From the perspective of the goals of archaeology, however, learning about how and why the ancestors of the Purisimeño Chumash became increasingly dependent on marine resources helps to fill a gap in knowledge of the range of prehistoric human adaptations to varying environmental situations, given that archaeology of coast-dwellers until recently has been rather descriptive and oftentimes pursued from an implicitly terrestrial perspective. Moreover, there are some great opportunities to contribute to a body of theory developing in archaeology concerned with accounting for the relative importance of different food resources included in the diet of a prehistoric population. As this case study demonstrates, some fertile empirical cases for assessing this growing body of theory can come from contrasts between marine and terrestrial food resources utilized by prehistoric coast-dwellers.

ACKNOWLEDGMENTS

An archaeological project the size and duration of the one that is the subject of this case study is a result of the efforts of many individuals, not only field and laboratory workers but also clerical assistants and other office workers concerned with administrative and logistical support. Although the number of these individuals is too large to include here all of their names—a few hundred altogether—they all have my sincere thanks for their diverse efforts and their commitment to fulfilling their assignments, sometimes under considerable time pressure and adverse working conditions. Several individuals should be singled out, however, for the key roles they played in the project. Dr. Pandora Snethkamp, who directed UCSB's Center for Archaeological Studies during the 1970s and 1980s, was my co-principal investigator, and she helped direct the 1978–80 field work. Representing the Chumash of the Santa Inez Indian Reservation during the 1974 field work was the late Juanita Centeno, who actually served as one of the field crew. Charlie Ochoa was our Chumash monitor during the 1978–80 field work. Finally, many individuals employed at Vandenberg Air Force Base helped with a myriad of logistical details during the field work, particularly with regard to room and board for the crew and access to facilities for field laboratories.

The U.S. Air Force Space Systems Division (formerly the Space and Missile Systems Organization) in Los Angeles provided funding for the various contracts under which the archaeological investigations were carried out. These contracts were administered for the Air Force by the Interagency Archaeological Services (IAS), a division of the National Park Service. IAS archaeologists Helene Dunbar and the late Garland Gordon made sure I fulfilled the terms of the contracts. Although we did not always agree, they were genuinely interested in my research on Vandenberg and helped in numerous ways to facilitate the fieldwork and laboratory analysis.

I wrote the first draft of this case study while on sabbatical leave from my teaching responsibilities at UCSB. My father-in-law Joe Ford, a retired sociology professor, generously allowed me to use his mountain cabin in order to get away from distractions of home and campus. About 150 miles from Santa Barbara in the small community of Wrightwood and without a phone, the cabin was an ideal getaway. My good Wrightwood friends Ken and Sandy Young ensured that I did not come down with cabin fever by having me over for dinner now and then. Otherwise known by his amateur radio call-sign NF6T, Ken occasionally would contact me on a two-meter amateur radio, and we would have lunch or a cup of coffee at a local Wrightwood eatery. My wife Anabel occasionally would phone Wrightwood neighbors Pat and Dick Home in an effort to reach me. Pat or Dick unhesitatingly would fetch me while Anabel waited on the line.

A number of people contributed in tangible ways to the preparation of this case study. Many of the illustrations for this case study were prepared by Dirk Brandts, Kirsten Olson, Dan Reeves, and Sara Gardiner. Mark Aldenderfer, a colleague in my department at UCSB, advised me on statistical matters and graphical displays of data. My colleagues Mike Moratto of Infotec Research, Inc., and Bob Bettinger of the UC Davis Department of Anthropology read and commented upon specific sections of an early draft of the case study. In his role as Series Editor, Jeff Quilter read the last drafts of this case study and provided many helpful comments. He also gave me a lot of encouragement during the course of writing. Jeff was especially well qualified as a reviewer because as a graduate student he was one of my crew chiefs during the 1974 investigations on Vandenberg, and he helped with the compilation of the resulting data.

My wife Anabel Ford, an archaeologist who studies the ancient Maya of Belize and Guatemala, frequently served as a sounding board for many of my ideas. Moreover, her emotional and material support has been critical, particularly during the stressful times when I was struggling to finish the final technical report for the Air Force and the National Park Service. Anabel also took the time to read and comment upon the penultimate draft of the case study.

CONTENTS

TABLES AND FIGURES

Tables

Figures

SERIES EDITOR
Jeffrey Quilter
Ripon College

PURISIMEÑO CHUMASH PREHISTORY

MARITIME ADAPTATIONS

ALONG THE SOUTHERN CALIFORNIA COAST

1

Introduction

SCOPE OF THIS STUDY

The prehistory of coastal California extends back in time at least 10,000 years, and by 8,000 years ago hunter-gatherer populations were large enough to have left behind a relatively rich archaeological record. Perhaps nowhere along the central California coast is this record as extensive and well preserved as on the large tract of land now encompassed by Vandenberg Air Force Base. Since the early 1970s the Air Force has funded several large archaeological projects that have dramatically increased our knowledge of the prehistory of the region dominated by the base, which for convenience I shall refer to as the Vandenberg region (Figure 1.1). I had the good fortune to have directed one of these projects, which entailed excavations at a number of sites in the southern portion of the base, known to locals as South Vandenberg. The sites from which I collected data are distributed through the whole 9,000 years of the region's prehistory; as a consequence I was able to address a number of research problems concerning the evolution of hunter-gatherer adaptations to a distinctive coastal environment.

My introduction to the rich archaeological resources of Vandenberg occurred in 1970, during my first year of teaching at the University of California at Santa Barbara. At that time, one of our graduate students, Larry Spanne, was engaged in a systematic survey of the base property, for which we eventually received some financial support from the Air Force via the National Park Service. These surveys provided the first indication of the large numbers of archaeological sites scattered throughout the base, and when planning began in 1973 for the construction of space shuttle launch facilities to complement those at Cape Canaveral, the Air Force realized that it must consider the prospect that construction of facilities could destroy archaeological sites.

In 1974 I was contracted by the National Park Service, with funding provided by the Air Force, to carry out an intensive survey of lands on the southern portion of the base on which space shuttle facilities might be built. In addition, I collected information through test excavations at 31 sites that stood the highest probability of being affected by construction activities to determine whether these sites were of sufficient significance to justify further attention. Because these excavations were the first in this region of coastal California—aside from a few poorly documented excavations by amateurs some decades earlier—my crew and I had little idea of what lay below the surface. As it turned out, several of the sites contained cultural deposits more

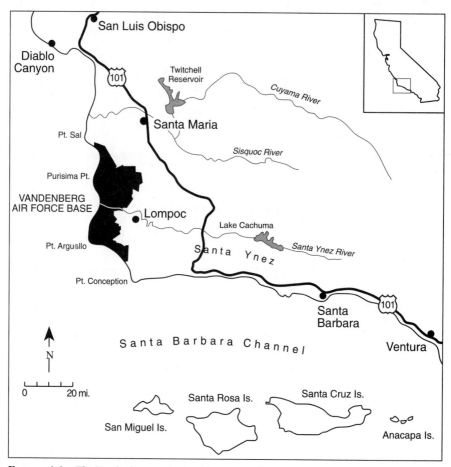

FIGURE 1.1   *The Vandenberg region and its geographic context.*

than 1.5 meters deep over more than 15 hectares (37 acres) of land. Even more surprising, two turned out to have deposits between 5 and 6 meters deep! Needless to say, we were overwhelmed by the amount of effort required to reach the base of the archaeological deposits at these sites.

The information collected in 1974 left little doubt that very significant archaeological resources could be affected by shuttle facilities construction. During the next few years, Air Force planners attempted to design the locations of facilities so as to avoid destruction of archaeological sites, and their efforts were largely successful. However, removal of portions of three sites could not reasonably be avoided. These three sites were situated along the edge of an existing highway that would have to be widened to serve as a route along which the shuttlecraft would be towed on a tractor trailer from the landing strip and the preparation facilities on the northern portion of the base to the launch facilities on the southern portion.

Consequently, the National Park Service contracted with me once again, this time to investigate those portions of the three sites that would be destroyed by the tow route widening. Under the contract, not only was I to excavate samples of the deposits to be destroyed but I was also to analyze the resulting data and prepare a report presenting the results of the analysis. Because so little was yet known about the prehistory of the region including the base, the contract provided for analysis of some of the collections obtained during the test excavations carried out in 1974 in order to enlarge the regional sample of data.

The bulk of the excavations was carried out over the late fall and winter of 1978–79. Although winter temperatures were relatively benign, as they typically are along the California coast, we had to cope with a good deal of rain and chilly wind. We would have preferred to wait until the next spring and summer to undertake the fieldwork, but the construction schedule required that we be finished by then. Some follow-up fieldwork had to be undertaken in 1980. Data analysis began in late 1985, and I submitted the final technical report to the National Park Service and the Air Force in 1990.

This case study concerns the project that began in 1978 but had its roots in the investigations carried out in 1974. For convenience, I shall refer to all archaeological investigations carried out in light of space shuttle development as the *Shuttle Project.* I have based the case study on my final technical report, but I also include new chronological information and further analyses of data in the technical report that I have published subsequently in several articles. As was the case with the technical report and the articles, my focus in this study is on subsistence change and its determinants. I am particularly concerned with the significance of marine food resources, including shellfish, sea mammals, and fish, and the way marine and terrestrial foods related to each other in a subsistence system. My efforts to discover the determinants of subsistence change have led me to consider the role of changes in regional population density and environmental conditions, but I also give some attention to the possible role of developing regional exchange systems.

In addition to presenting my analysis of subsistence change, I provide some idea of the context of my research on Vandenberg. Archaeological research performed under contract has its peculiarities, which are largely a product of how laws and guidelines govern when and how archaeological investigations should be performed. I do not mean to imply that constraints on my Vandenberg research were particularly onerous, but an appreciation of certain aspects of my research design does require an understanding of the legal and administrative context of contract-funded research.

THE VANDENBERG REGION'S ENVIRONMENTAL SETTING

The geographic division between central and southern California generally is considered to be a prominent "corner" along the California coast known as Point Conception (Figure 1.1). East of Point Conception is the 100-km-long Santa Barbara Channel, whose quiet waters harbor a rich and accessible marine fauna. North of the point the coastline is exposed to the full brunt of prevailing winds from the northwest, and the surf is generally so strong as to frustrate launching of small boats and to make swimming dangerous. Because this stretch of coastline is west-facing, winds drive beach sands inland to form some of the most extensive dunefields along the Pacific coast of

North America. During the summer months, cool fogs frequently hang over this coastline, and during the winter months northwesterly winds reaching velocities of 30 to 50 miles per hour often follow winter rainstorms. Annual temperature variations are not extreme due to the ameliorating effect of the ocean. Average summer temperatures range between 60°F and 63°F (typically never higher than 74°F) and average winter temperatures between 51°F and 53°F (typically never lower than 38°F). Most precipitation occurs during the winter months between November and March. At Santa Maria, a city north and inland from the base, annual precipitation averages 12.35 inches (31 cm). Only very rarely does it snow at or near the coast.

The Vandenberg coastline offers spectacular scenery, especially on clear days when points of land can be seen in the distance jutting into the dark blue ocean. These points of land were significant to aboriginal settlement in that they typically are associated with extensive rocky intertidal zones from which shellfish could be collected, and their lee, or southerly, sides offered some protection from heavy surf and prevailing wind. In the southern extreme of Vandenberg, Point Arguello is the last major point before Point Conception, 22 km to the southeast. Several of the sites clustering near Point Arguello were subjects of my research on South Vandenberg. The south-facing lee of this point is approximately 12 km long, and in a protected locality along this lee are the two largest sites known to exist in the region. Near the center of the Vandenberg coast is Purisima Point. Very extensive archaeological

PHOTO 1.1   *The coastline south of Point Arguello. Bedrock shelves visible above the surf are prime habitats for California mussel, black turban, and other shellfish. Rocky Point, the prominent headland in the distance, is partly shrouded by fog.*

deposits also exist here. Finally, just beyond the northern boundary of the base is Point Sal. I documented the cluster of sites at the tip of this point for the Bureau of Land Management, which owns approximately 70 acres there.

Because of wind and fog, the Vandenberg coast is not hospitable, and in fact modern-day communities in the region, Lompoc and Santa Maria being the largest, are located several miles inland, where climatic conditions are more benign. Why, then, was this coastal region so popular aboriginally? Some of the largest sites in California, in terms of volume of deposits, occur within a few hundred meters of the South Vandenberg coast, and the coastal zone as a whole has some of the highest densities of archaeological sites found in North America. The reason for the coast's attraction during aboriginal times clearly is the abundance of marine fauna that served as a plentiful source of food. California mussels, in particular, are prolific in the rocky intertidal zones along the Vandenberg coast, and fragments of their shells are a prevalent constituent of the site deposits.

Although California mussel *(Mytilus californianus)* is the most abundant shellfish in the rocky intertidal zones, a variety of smaller mollusks also are available and were collected. Among these are the black turban *(Tegula funebralis)*, a marine snail that is perhaps as abundant in the rocky intertidal zone as California mussels. Bedrock shelves extending into the intertidal zone, as well as offshore rocks, also are

PHOTO 1.2   *A typical bed of California mussels exposed at low tide. California mussels often are so dense that the bedrock surface to which they are attached cannot be seen.*

popular haulouts used by harbor seals *(Phoca vitulina)* and California sea lions *(Zalophus californianus)*. Nearshore waters contain a variety of fish that could be obtained with hook-and-line or nets. Surfperch *(Amphistichus* spp.), rockfish *(Sebastes* spp.), and cabezon *(Scorpaenichthys marmoratus)* are some of the more common species. In general, however, fishing would have been constrained by the frequently heavy surf and the inability to use small watercraft. Nonetheless, fishing and sea mammal hunting are indicated by the presence of their bones in site deposits.

Terrestrial resources are relatively limited. Plant communities near the coast typically are dominated by coastal sage and other low chaparral shrubs, often growing so densely as to frustrate passage on foot. Aside from firewood, these plants offer few resources of use to aboriginal peoples. Grasslands occurring in locations relatively protected from the prevailing wind do contain a number of plants bearing edible seeds. Significantly, oaks are extremely rare within 10 km of the coast. Elsewhere in California, acorns from a variety of species of oaks were a major stored food resource, so their absence near the coast in the Vandenberg region has strong implications with regard to aboriginal subsistence and settlement systems. The chaparral vegetation harbors relatively abundant mule deer *(Odocoileus hemionus),* blacktail jackrabbits *(Lepus californicus),* and brush rabbits *(Sylvilagus bachmani),* and their bones in the site deposits testify to their importance as food resources.

The availability of fresh water, of course, is basic to human settlement. In general, aboriginal inhabitants of the Vandenberg coast had little problem obtaining fresh water. Springs occur within or adjacent to a number of small canyons and ravines, and several streams are perennial. On South Vandenberg, Honda Creek has by far the largest watershed and obviously would have provided a highly reliable water supply (Figure 3.1). Dividing North and South Vandenberg is the Santa Ynez River, which has a watershed extending 120 km inland. Although perennial, it becomes a true river only during winter months after rains have had a significant effect on its watershed. At the mouth of the Santa Ynez River are an extensive saltmarsh and a tidal lagoon, the latter becoming an important resource area late in prehistory.

I mentioned earlier the coastal dunes, which give most of the Vandenberg coastal lands a distinctive hilly topography. In some localities, especially near the mouth of the Santa Ynez River, relatively large dunes of fresh, white beach sand are forming today. However, dunes immediately landward from the coast are clearly older. Their surfaces are covered with scrub vegetation, and the color of the sand is a rich orange-tan, in sharp contrast to the white beach sand. On South Vandenberg, dunes stabilized by a mantle of vegetation and still retaining fresh dune topography form a belt between the mouth of the Santa Ynez River and Honda Canyon. Extending inland from the edge of the seacliff approximately 500 meters, these dunes are known to be of "Intermediate" age in a dune chronology developed by a geologist. (Figure 3.1 shows the location of this dune belt.) Stratigraphically beneath this Intermediate dune belt and extending inland beyond it are much older dunes that have lost most of their distinctive topography through erosion. These are known as "Old" in the dune chronology. The surface of the Old dunes has been stable long enough for an organic soil to develop; such soils have not yet developed to an appreciable extent on the superimposed Intermediate dunes. My colleague Don Johnson, a geographer specializing in coastal geomorphology and soils, estimates that the Intermediate dunes are only about 2,000 years old, whereas the Old dunes probably are in excess of 5,000 years old. The date for the formation of the Intermediate dunes actually is based on archaeological information. Exposed along the face of a road cut just north of Honda Canyon are two archaeological deposits, one consisting of a stratum of cultural deposits between the Old and Intermediate dunes with radiocarbon dates between 3400 and 4800 B.P. and the other on top of the Intermediate dunes with radiocarbon dates between 500 B.P. and 600 B.P. Thus the Intermediate dunes must have formed sometime between 3400 B.P. and 600 B.P. (I shall discuss these deposits further in Chapter 5). Only neighboring site SBA-530 is known to have similar stratification of archaeological and dune deposits, and we can only speculate about how many other sites are completely obscured by sand dunes.

It is indeed fortunate that the function of Vandenberg Air Force Base has fostered indirectly a large degree of preservation of the archaeological sites scattered throughout the 39,900 ha (98,600 acres) of the base property. The base is devoted to launching satellites into polar orbits along southerly trajectories over the Pacific Ocean, as well as testing various military missile systems. Because missile launch facilities must be separated by extensive "clear zones," large tracts of natural wildlands exist throughout the base. As a result, abundant and well-preserved archaeological resources on the base offer archaeologists opportunities to study coastal hunter-gatherer adaptations and cultural change that are largely unparalleled in California.

THE VANDENBERG REGION'S ARCHAEOLOGICAL SITES

More than 800 archaeological sites currently are known to exist on Vandenberg property, and many parts of the base have yet to be thoroughly surveyed. Indeed, site density is so high throughout most of the Vandenberg region that a person standing at any given spot is likely no more than a few hundred meters from a site. As one might expect, however, sites vary considerably in size and characteristics of their deposits. Two of the sites included in this analysis have deposits more than 5 meters deep, which ranks them among the deepest in California. But the Vandenberg region also contains many very small sites, the smallest consisting of only a few chert flakes or pieces of shell within an area a couple of meters square. The region's high site density and particularly the abundance of relatively small sites (less than 50 m in diameter) undoubtedly are products of two factors: a very long prehistory and relatively high mobility of social units.

Sites at or near the coast typically contain abundant shellfish remains, usually more than 80 percent of which is California mussel. In a few coastal sites shellfish remains appear to contribute at least 50 percent of the volume of archaeological deposits, but usually the percentage is closer to 10 percent. Most shell-bearing sites—frequently called *shell middens*—also contain bones of land mammals, sea mammals, fish, and birds. The abundance of vertebrate bones is never close to that of shell, which often blankets the surface of shell midden sites and makes them very easy to identify during a survey. As shall be seen later in this study, however, the relative scarcity of bone is deceiving.

In contrast to sites with substantial deposits of shell midden, many sites in all parts of the region consist mainly of a scatter of chert flakes, this type of site being most visible in dune blowouts. A type of banded chert occurs throughout the region in shale bedrock outcrops and as beach and stream cobbles, and the abundance of knapping waste in most Vandenberg sites seems to reflect a rather liberal use of this raw material for manufacture of projectile points, knives, and expediently shaped tools for cutting and scraping. Where dune sand has been blown away to expose a once-buried scatter of chert flakes, sometimes individual episodes of knapping may be observed in the form of a cluster of flakes, all obviously derived from one core, which may be present as well.

The larger and deeper sites in the region generally have a sandy loam soil matrix that is dark brown to gray in color, whereas soils surrounding these sites are usually light to medium brown in color. The dark soil color is caused by carbon from hearth fires and organic refuse, but hearths themselves almost never are preserved. In fact, structural features of any sort are difficult to discern. In addition, soil stratification frequently is absent or at least quite vague, even though radiocarbon dates from some of the larger sites indicate multiple occupations over several hundred or even several thousand years. Nonetheless, test excavations at a number of sites have revealed that stratigraphic distinctions do occur, and some of these are associated with surfaces that may be house floors. Investigation of such features, however, would be a major undertaking due to the volume of overlying midden deposits that must be excavated to expose them.

Aside from chert flakes and other knapping debris, artifacts generally are relatively rare in sites of the Vandenberg region, averaging perhaps under five per cubic meter of deposits. However, in sites dating before 5000 B.P. seed-milling implements actually may average several per cubic meter. Other classes of artifacts always are much rarer. Typical kinds of artifacts occurring in Vandenberg sites are fragments of projectile points and knives, chert flakes with retouched edges, mortar and pestle fragments, bone point fragments, shell beads (particularly in late prehistoric sites), and shell fishhook fragments. Because most of these artifacts are in low densities in site deposits, relatively large volumes must be excavated to obtain quantities sufficient for quantitative analysis. In only a few instances during my research in the Vandenberg region was I able to obtain quantities of artifacts appropriate for the more sophisticated approaches to quantitative analysis available to archaeologists.

The depositional characteristics of Vandenberg sites, except some of those in dunes, have been profoundly influenced by the burrowing activities of the pocket gopher (*Thomomys bottae*). Gophers have dug industriously through archaeological sites that may have been occupied two or three separate times during the course of prehistory. As a result, the strata produced by each occupation became so mixed that they no longer can be differentiated. Not uncommonly, gophers have burrowed through more than 50 percent of a site's volume, and in sites several thousand years old the percentage may be much higher. Evidence of gopher burrowing takes the form of *krotovina*, the soil-filled burrows seen in cross-section on excavation unit walls. Frequently the soil filling the burrows is lighter or darker in color than the

PHOTO 1.3   *A discrete concentration of chert flakes, cores, and hammerstones on a dune surface. Such concentrations may represent a knapping episode lasting only 15 minutes.*

PHOTO 1.4   *The floor of an excavation unit at site SBA-931 showing numerous krotovina. The light-colored deposits are mainly sterile soil into which gophers burrowed. Their tunnels then filled with darker soil from above, creating krotovina. Note that the clarity of the kroto-vina varies from very distinct to barely discernible, the variation being a result of both age and the proportions of darker and lighter soils in the krotovina. On the wall profile, the upper cultural stratum is represented by the dark soil, whereas the lower cultural stratum is close to the color of the sterile soil. The latter is not easily distinguished from sterile soil in this photograph.*

surrounding soil, but frequently the color differences are very subtle, leading me to suspect that many more krotovina exist than are possible to observe, particularly in sites several thousand years old.

Only within the last 15 years have archaeologists working in California come to grips with just how extensive the mixing of archaeological deposits by gophers has been (Erlandson 1984; Bocek 1986; Johnson 1989). Earlier, some archaeologists naive to the effects of rodent burrowing assumed that a site with no apparent stratification of cultural deposits represented one occupation lasting only a short time or a continuous occupation over many hundreds, if not thousands, of years. Consequently, many cultural changes have been viewed as a series of gradual transformations. As shall be seen when we consider the results of my research, compensating for the effects of gopher burrowing on the archaeological record is a difficult task. In many instances these effects are simply too great to overcome. Because I am aware of the potential effects of gopher burrowing, however, I know when to say that certain interpretations must be tentative.

SIGNIFICANCE OF THE RESEARCH

It is common for archaeologists to justify their research by referring to the inadequate prior knowledge of a region's prehistory. Given that one of the generally accepted goals of archaeology is to reconstruct prehistory, this justification is valid. But reconstructing prehistory should never be the only motivation for field research. With regard to my research objectives, certainly I recognized that little was known about the prehistory of the Vandenberg region. Indeed, the region had witnessed only one systematic archaeological excavation followed by data analysis and reporting. However, I also recognized that we still knew very little about hunter-gatherer adaptations in coastal settings, particularly with regard to how they developed through prehistory and the determinants of cultural change. I felt an obligation, therefore, to make a contribution to archaeology's general comparative knowledge of coastal hunter-gatherers, as well as to the growing body of theory concerning the causes of cultural change among prehistoric hunter-gatherers in general.

Surveys carried out in the early 1970s had indicated that some sites probably were quite old, based on the presence on site surfaces of certain artifact types known to be relatively ancient in the adjoining Santa Barbara Channel region and in the coastal locality 40 km north of Vandenberg near the mouth of Diablo Canyon. I suspected, therefore, that there was the opportunity to study cultural change of coastal hunter-gatherers over relatively long periods of time, on the order of several thousand years. As it turned out, the testing program in 1974 revealed that archaeological deposits at three sites were nearly 8,000 years old and that other deposits dated to a series of later phases of prehistory. Given that the dated deposits differed with regard to prevalent artifact types, as well as to proportions of different categories of faunal remains, I realized at the completion of our preliminary evaluation of the 1974 data that indeed the opportunity to study cultural change existed.

During my first visits to coastal sites in the Vandenberg region, I was struck by the much higher densities of shellfish remains in these sites in comparison to densities in sites along the Santa Barbara Channel mainland. Clearly Vandenberg aboriginal populations were much more dependent on shellfish than were their neighbors living along the mainland coast of the Santa Barbara Channel. I reasoned that the much greater prevalence of California mussel living in the intertidal zones along the Vandenberg coast must somehow underlie the differences in dependence on shellfish, but I suspected that the full explanation surely was more complicated than this. At the same time, I wondered about the validity of Osborn's argument that shellfish were a very labor-intensive food resource that would be exploited only if other food resources, particularly terrestrial as opposed to marine resources, were in short supply (Osborn 1977). It seemed to me that I could evaluate Osborn's argument through comparison between the contexts of shellfish in the subsistence systems of the Santa Barbara Channel and those of the Vandenberg region.

For some years prior to the Shuttle Project I had been interested in the role of population growth as an underlying factor affecting culture change. I felt that the increasing complexity in subsistence technology and social organization and the increasing diversity of subsistence resources seen through the prehistory of the neighboring Santa Barbara Channel region was somehow related to increasing population density. In this regard, I was inspired not only by earlier research I had carried out in the American Southwest but also by research of some of my colleagues in California. In later years I also began to be concerned about the role of long-term environmental fluctuations in affecting the course of cultural change. This interest was fostered by two paleoenvironmental reconstructions spanning the last 8,000-plus years that pertain to the Santa Barbara Channel region. Both reconstructions were based on high-resolution data obtained from a varved sediment core extracted from the bottom of the Santa Barbara Channel. These reconstructions revealed that sea water temperature (and therefore air temperature) and vegetation communities had varied significantly during the course of the Holocene (the geological epoch following the Ice Age, or Pleistocene Epoch). By the completion of the excavations in 1980, I felt that the archaeological data from the Shuttle Project could be used to address the dual roles of human population and environmental fluctuations in influencing the course of cultural change. This research objective obviously is very general, but it seemed appropriate given the long spans of time and the degree of chronological resolution represented in the Shuttle Project data.

It is these three problem areas—the nature of cultural change, the dietary significance of shellfish, and the effects of change in human population numbers and paleoenvironment—that guided my research on South Vandenberg. I should emphasize, however, that my thinking about these problems evolved through the course of the project as I became more familiar with the data available for analysis and as information and ideas became available in the archaeological and paleoenvironmental literature. As I began the Shuttle Project in 1974, my research problems were only very crudely formulated, and I was relatively more concerned with learning something about the nature of the archaeological record of the Vandenberg region. As I learned more about the region's archaeological record, I began to recognize its applicability to addressing a wide variety of research problems concerned with variability in hunter-gatherer adaptations in both time and space.

2

Prehistoric and Ethnographic
Background

CULTURES AT THE TIME OF EUROPEAN CONTACT

For purposes of archaeology, ethnohistoric and ethnographic information is invaluable as a basis for making sense of the archaeological record, even during earlier periods of prehistory when cultural systems clearly were different from those that existed when Europeans first visited the region. The most ideal would be detailed ethnohistoric accounts of cultural systems in the Vandenberg region at the time of European contact in the late 1700s. Alternatively, we would be satisfied with diverse ethnographic information pertaining to a historic period during which many aspects of the aboriginal culture still existed or were remembered. Regrettably, both bodies of information are very sketchy. There are brief ethnohistoric accounts in the form of journal entries by members of Spanish expeditions traveling through the region in the late eighteenth century, and a good deal of genealogical information was recorded by Franciscan missionaries, who obtained it from natives brought into the local missions. There is extremely little ethnographic information pertaining specifically to aboriginal populations of the Vandenberg region, although a good deal does exist for the neighboring regions of the middle Santa Ynez Valley and the Santa Barbara Channel. The following sketch of Vandenberg region aboriginal culture, more or less at the time of European contact, is based on all these sources of information.

The Vandenberg region falls within the area occupied by the Chumash people. The term *Chumash* actually refers to a family of three distinct but closely related languages spoken by populations living in villages along the California coast from the modern-day community of Malibu (derived from the native name of a Chumash village at the same location) near Los Angeles, northward through the Santa Barbara Channel and the Vandenberg region, to the vicinity of the city of San Luis Obispo. Inland-dwelling Chumash occupied the mountains and valleys as much as 68 km from the coast (Figure 2.1). Chumash villages also existed on the Channel Islands forming the southern edge of the Santa Barbara Channel. The total Chumash-speaking population is estimated to have been approximately 18,500 (Cook 1976:37–38).

The Chumash occupying the Vandenberg region are known as the Purisimeño, this designation being derived from the name of the nearest Spanish Mission, La Purísima Concepción, located near the city of Lompoc (Greenwood 1978). Purisimeño villages were distributed from the western Santa Barbara Channel northward through the Vandenberg region to a point a short distance north of the Santa Maria River. The Purisimeño occupied approximately 22 villages in all. Although Purisimeño and other

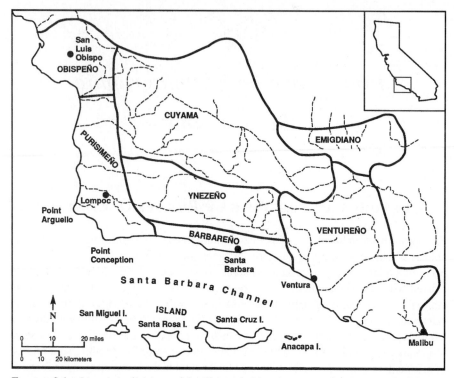

FIGURE 2.1   *Linguistic divisions of the Chumash. Linguists currently question whether these traditionally recognized linguistic divisions give a true picture of Chumash languages. Some recognize only three Chumash languages:* Northern *(Obispeño),* Central *(Purisimeño, Barbareño, Ynezeño, Cuyama, Ventureño, and Emigdiano), and* Island. *With regard to the Central Chumash language, dialectical divisions may correlate with some of the original divisions, but dialectical variations are poorly understood.*

Chumash settlements are commonly referred to as "villages" in the literature, the number of people living in one settlement was much smaller than this term implies. Purisimeño settlements ranged between 30 and 200 (King 1984, Table 5b), and the largest Chumash settlements, located along the Santa Barbara Channel near the city of Santa Barbara, had populations between 500 and 800 (Brown 1967; King 1971). Spanish missionaries and settlers called native settlements throughout California "rancherias," a term more appropriate to the typical population size of settlements in native California than the conventionally used term "village."

   Two Purisimeño villages existed on South Vandenberg: *Nocto,* located east of Point Arguello and the subject of testing in 1974; and *Lompoc,* located in the Santa Ynez Valley somewhere just west of the modern-day city of Lompoc, named for the nearby Purisimeño village. Considering the high density of archaeological sites on South Vandenberg, one might wonder why there were only two documented villages when Mission La Purísima Concepción was established in 1787. The reason is that the sites of these villages were not the only ones occupied during the year. Typical of hunter-gatherers the world over, the Purisimeño Chumash also occupied a series of temporary camps during the course of a given year for purposes of acquiring food resources and provisions from the immediate vicinity of each camp. The villages of Nocto and Lompoc were the principal settlements, and if the ethnohistoric information pertaining to Santa Barbara Channel villages (Landberg 1965) may be applied to Purisimeño villages as well, these two villages probably were occupied principally during the winter months.

Only one ethnohistoric account gives any indication of the nature of Purisimeño mobility patterns. When the Portolá expedition passed through North Vandenberg in late August of 1769 on its way north, it encountered an encampment of Purisimeño Chumash without houses, which implies that this camp was relatively temporary. When they returned in January 1770, the camp was abandoned. Unfortunately, this is the only account providing such information, but because the Portolá expedition also visited some of the named Purisimeño villages that did have houses, one may surmise that during late summer at least some Purisimeño were away from their main settlements and apparently were relatively mobile.

In order to gain a basic understanding of Purisimeño Chumash culture, it will help to compare what little is known to the better-documented culture of the Chumash living along the central Santa Barbara Channel. Anthropologists have designated the Chumash living along the mainland coast of the channel the Barbareño and Ventureño (again, taking their names from the nearest missions, Santa Bárbara and San Buenaventura). They also spoke the Central Chumash language, although there appears to have been a distinct dialectical division between the two. The Chumash living on the other side of the channel, on the northern Channel Islands, spoke the Island Chumash language. The Barbareño, coastal Ventureño, and Island Chumash lived in relatively large coastal villages (Figure 2.2), the greater proportion having populations of more than 150 individuals (King 1971). Their subsistence was based on relatively intensive fishing in the nearshore waters using hook-and-line, nets, and harpoons. They also hunted seals and sea lions, but terrestrial hunting apparently was not very important. Offshore fishing was from the distinctive *tomol,* a canoe made of wood planks lashed together at intervals along their margins and caulked with tar. Gathering plant foods also was important, and acorns were a major stored food resource as was the case in many other parts of California.

Each channel village was headed by at least one headman or chief. Chiefs inherited their positions within elite families who controlled a good deal of wealth and may have been the principal individuals who owned plank canoes. Assisting a village chief was a series of officials who also were of high social status. Villages were politically autonomous, although various ethnohistoric and ethnographic data imply that alliances or federations between neighboring villages existed and that a chief of a relatively large village may have exerted political influence, in some cases reinforced by military dominance, over chiefs of neighboring villages. In general, however, multivillage organization appears to have been relatively tenuous and to have been based on either economic exchange relationships or military alliance (Johnson 1988:125; King 1990:58).

Santa Barbara Channel Chumash society was stratified, consisting minimally of elite and commoner families. Craft specialists, who made plank canoes and other items of technology, apparently were in intermediate status positions (King 1990:59).

FIGURE 2.2   *An artist's reconstruction of a Chumash village. Drawn by Adan Treganza, this view shows thatched hemispherical houses distributed just above the beach, a typical location of villages along the Santa Barbara Channel. Plank canoes are drawn onto the beach, and a canoe paddle leans against the house in the foreground. A large stone mortar and pestle are beside the house's entrance, and baskets and abalone shell dishes are in the immediate foreground.*

Although ethnographic data are vague with regard to how kinship was used to define social groups and social relations, an analysis of genealogical information derived from baptismal, marriage, and death registers kept by the Franciscan missionaries indicates that Chumash villages of the Santa Barbara Channel region were matrilocal, with the husband moving to the village of his wife upon marriage. This pattern and various clues in the ethnographic and ethnohistoric literature imply that lineage groups within a village probably were matrilineal. The genealogical data also reveal that chiefs frequently departed from this matrilocal pattern in that they resided in their natal village after marriage, although they may have resided in their wife's village before ascending to chiefdom. Moreover, a chief generally had more than one wife, and these wives typically were from villages with whom he apparently wished to maintain alliances. Interestingly, some wives of chiefs appear to have continued to live in their natal villages and therefore would see their husband only when he visited their village (Johnson 1988:170–179).

The exchange economy entailed the use of shell-bead money, which took the form of strings of small, disk-shaped beads made from shells of the purple olive (*Olivella biplicata*), a small marine snail. (Archaeologists generally use the genus name *Olivella* as a common name.) As well, high-status individuals measured their wealth in terms of amounts of shell-bead money. Practically all of the shell-bead money was made by Chumash living on the Channel Islands across the Santa Barbara Channel (King 1971; Arnold 1992a:73–74). Indeed archaeological sites on the Channel Islands occupied in late prehistoric and protohistoric times contain abundant shell refuse from bead making, along with discarded and broken stone tips of drills used to perforate the beads. The shell-bead money was used throughout Chumash territory to facilitate exchange of food products, many kinds of craft items, and raw materials (King 1971). In particular, there was an active trade between villages on either side of the Santa Barbara Channel using the plank canoe for cross-channel transportation. Interestingly, once the missions were established, the value of shell-bead money could be given in terms of the Spanish monetary system. Also of interest is the fact that the shell-bead money made and used by the Chumash eventually reached the hands of their neighbors, such as the Gabrielino, who occupied the Los Angeles Basin, and the Yokuts, who occupied the San Joaquin Valley northeast of Chumash territory. Moreover, Chumash money and other shell products have been found in sites as far away as southern Nevada and Arizona.

In contrast to the Barbareño and Ventureño Chumash living along the Santa Barbara Channel coast, the Purisimeño living north of Point Conception did not use plank canoes, undoubtedly because the craft was not well adapted to rough surf and choppy waters. This meant that any fishing had to be done from shore and therefore would not have been as productive. Shellfish collecting appears to have compensated to some extent for less dependence on fishing. Despite differences in subsistence practices, the various items of technology for acquiring and processing food resources and raw materials probably were essentially the same.

Status differentiation similar to that found in the large Santa Barbara Channel villages appears also to have existed among the Purisimeño. However, the mission registers contain only one specific reference to a village chief among the Purisimeño, in contrast to frequent references to chiefs of Santa Barbara Channel villages. The registers do reveal that a Purisimeño village typically contained at least one man with more than one wife, a typical situation among Santa Barbara Channel chiefs but not among commoners (King 1984:I41–I43). It may be that the office of village headman was not as well defined among the Purisimeño as it was among the Santa Barbara Channel Chumash. In fact, it is possible that Purisimeño political organization was more of a "big man" type, in which political leadership shifted between individuals relatively frequently, depending on one's fortunes at the moment. This seemingly greater fluidity in political organization is reflected in marriage patterns. Mission register data indicate that a newly married Purisimeño couple might reside in the village of either the husband's or the wife's family (King 1984:I47). This implies that matrilineal organization may not have existed among the Purisimeño.

The popular literature describing Chumash culture has assumed frequently, often implicitly, that all Chumash people participated in essentially one type of culture, that is, the culture of those Chumash living in the central part of their territory to which the bulk of the ethnohistoric and ethnographic information pertains. The comparison between the Santa Barbara Channel Chumash and the Purisimeño Chumash just presented reveals that this was not the case. The Purisimeño surely did not have the same complex political organization found among the Santa Barbara Channel villages, and their social organization was not as structured. These differences probably relate in part to the Purisimeños' not depending on the plank canoe, which required the expenditure of a good deal of wealth to construct, and perhaps also to their more dispersed and more mobile settlement pattern. Nonetheless, the Purisimeño and other Chumash groups were linked together in a interregional exchange network facilitated by the use of shell-bead money.

Obviously archaeological data can help to flesh out the manner in which Purisimeño culture differed from that of other Chumash groups, in particular the Chumash living along the Santa Barbara Channel. Accordingly, I attempted to address two research questions pertaining to likely differences. First, I was concerned with elucidating the subsistence differences between the Purisimeño and the Santa Barbara Channel Chumash and the factors underlying these differences. Second, I hoped to determine what the Purisimeño contributed to the interregional exchange, that is, what they provided in exchange for shell-bead money.

Prehistoric Background

Until the Shuttle Project and a series of subsequent archaeological projects on Vandenberg (Chambers Consultants and Planners 1984; Woodman et al. 1991), the bulk of archaeological research in Chumash territory had taken place at sites along the central Santa Barbara Channel and the Channel Islands. As a result, much of what we know about Chumash prehistory pertains to the Santa Barbara Channel. Sporadic work elsewhere in Chumash territory indicates broad similarities in sequences of artifact forms, but with few exceptions little effort has been devoted to determining what differences might exist in the prehistories of different regions of Chumash territory. Given this state of affairs, it makes sense to begin with an outline of Santa Barbara Channel prehistory and then consider what variations are known to exist, or would be expected to exist, in other regions of Chumash territory.

As is true of most regions of North America, the beginnings of prehistory are only tentatively known. During the 1950s and 1960s, Phil Orr (1956, 1968) reported that he discovered evidence of late Pleistocene occupation on Santa Rosa Island, one of the Channel Islands along the southern margin of the Santa Barbara Channel, by people who hunted pygmy mammoths that roamed the Channel Islands until about 10,000–11,000 years ago. My colleagues and I have since demonstrated that the alleged roasting pits where mammoth meat supposedly was cooked were products of ancient forest fires or other natural processes. Although there is a possibility of occupation on the Channel Islands as early as 9,000 years ago, there are currently no data indicating that the pygmy mammoths and humans were on the islands at the same time.

More definitive evidence of late Pleistocene occupation of the Santa Barbara Channel region is a small basal fragment of a Clovis point obtained from the surface of a coastal site (Erlandson et al. 1987). Clovis points are known to date between about 11,000 B.P. and 12,000 B.P. in other parts of North America, but no datable material was in clear association with the Santa Barbara Channel point fragment. Indeed, it is possible that someone collected the point several thousand years later from a known center of Clovis activity such as the edge of Tulare Lake, located 150 km to the northeast, and brought it to the Santa Barbara Channel.

A site on San Miguel Island, the westernmost of the Channel Islands, has yielded a radiocarbon date of 10,300 B.P., but little information is yet available regarding the context of this date. However, midden deposits directly above the stratum from which the shell sample for this date was collected are associated with radiocarbon dates in excess of 8000 B.P. Even if the 10,300 B.P. date were eventually rejected, this site is the earliest so far known in the Santa Barbara Channel region (Erlandson 1991:108).

A relatively large number of sites dating between about 8000 B.P. and 6500 B.P. appear to reflect the first widespread occupation of the Santa Barbara Channel coast. These sites typically contain relatively high densities of seed-milling implements, specifically metates (millingstones) and manos (handstones; Figure 2.3). The type of metate found in early southern California sites typically is a slab of sandstone with a shallow-to-deep ovoid depression resulting from abrasion against manos in the course of milling seeds into flour. Two implications may be derived from the abundance of these milling implements in sites of this age. First, seeds appear to have been dietarily important. Second, if seeds were stored for future consumption, which seems likely, the sites where they were milled and consumed probably were residential bases. Remains of seeds have never been recovered from sites of this antiquity, in large part because preservation of such fragile items as carbonized seeds is very poor. Most likely a wide variety of small seeds of grasses and annuals were collected.

Diet appears to have been quite diverse during this early prehistoric period. Mollusk shells, bones of various terrestrial and marine mammals, and nearshore fish indicate that all major categories of fauna were exploited. Mollusks appear to have been dietarily more important than mammals and fish, and most were obtained from estuaries at the mouths of streams along the Santa Barbara Channel coast (Erlandson 1994). Other food resources and various raw materials such as plant fibers probably were obtained from these estuaries, which were created at the end of the Pleistocene as a result of relatively rapid sea-level rise drowning the mouths of coastal canyons. Only vestiges of these estuaries exist today.

Other than milling implements, artifacts from sites of this age are relatively nondescript. A variety of randomly shaped flaked stone tools, many of coarse-grained local rocks such as quartzite, probably were used in a variety of cutting and chopping tasks. Projectile points are rare and are not of distinctive shapes, which is curious given that hunting clearly was an important subsistence activity. Hammerstones frequently are quite abundant, and most appear to have been used to pit the surfaces of milling implements to maintain their milling effectiveness. Fish were caught with baited hooks, the simplest being a gorge. This was a straight piece of bone three to five centimeters long and pointed at both ends, with a line attached around the middle. True hooks consisted of two bone pieces lashed together such that one piece served as the shank and the other as the barb (King 1990:80, 231; Figure 2.3).

Mortuary practices inferred from artifacts associated with burials of this period indicate that society was primarily egalitarian. Nonetheless, some individuals may have been in leadership positions of high status, but, if so, these positions probably were achieved during one's lifetime rather than having been ascribed at birth. Shell beads and ornaments (Figure 2.3) are relatively common mortuary goods, but their quantities are far smaller than was the case later in prehistory. Their presence in cemeteries at least 7,000 years old is the beginning of a tradition persisting until

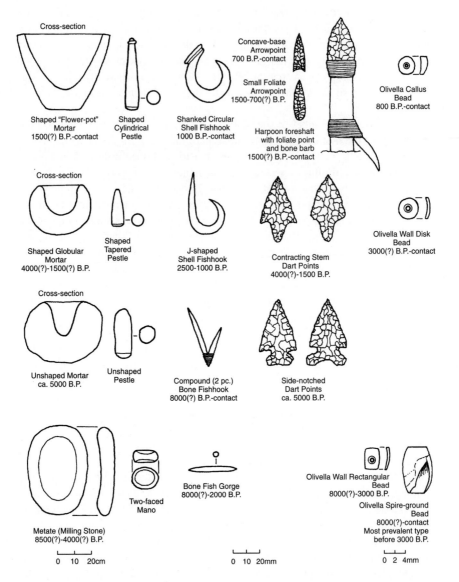

FIGURE 2.3 *Typical artifacts of the Vandenberg and neighboring regions. These are among the most distinctive artifacts found in sites of these two regions; as a result, they often are used in cross-dating. The date or time interval associated with each artifact form is the approximate period during which the artifact form was made.*

aboriginal Chumash cultural systems became extinct during the historic period. At this early time, however, shell beads did not serve the important economic functions characteristic of the late prehistoric period.

In addition to the mainland coast, the Channel Islands also have yielded a good deal of evidence of occupation during the 8000 B.P.–6500 B.P. time interval. Milling implements are very rare in island sites of this age, implying that seeds were not as important a resource on the islands. Instead, digging sticks weighted with stones pecked and ground into the shape and size of a doughnut were used to dig up bulbs or tubers. The difference in plant food emphasis between the islands and mainland probably was due to reduced availability of appropriate seed-bearing plants on the islands. To compensate for the lack of game animals, marine fauna, especially California mussels, were dietarily more important on the islands than along the Channel mainland coast (Glassow 1993).

Occupation of the Channel Islands implies that people somehow crossed the 20-plus miles of the Santa Barbara Channel using some sort of boat. If in fact occupation on the Channel Islands is as old as 10,000 years, one can infer that some of the earliest inhabitants of California used some sort of watercraft. The easiest to construct probably would have been a raft made of bundles of bulrush stalks, but it is also possible that dugout canoes were used. The Chumash used both at the time of European contact as vessels supplementing their plank canoes (Hudson et al. 1978). Regardless of the type of craft first used to cross the channel, it is apparent that contact between the mainland and islands was continual, in light of the presence in island sites of artifacts made of materials from mainland sources, obsidian projectile points being an obvious example.

There is comparatively little evidence of occupation in the Santa Barbara Channel region between about 6500 and about 5000 B.P., which I have attributed to decreased productivity of food resources brought about by a long, arid climatic interval frequently called the Altithermal (Glassow et al. 1988). During this period regional population density appears to have been quite low, but beginning around 5000 B.P. the marked increase in the number of sites implies that population density reached at least the level achieved prior to 6500 B.P. In addition, a significant change in milling technology occurred about 5000 B.P., this being the introduction of the stone mortar and pestle. Mortars at this time were large, unshaped cobbles into which a subconical hole was pecked (Figure 2.3). The pestle, an elongate cobble roughly cylindrical in shape, was plunged into the hole to pulverize a food product.

Ethnographic data from different groups in California indicate that while metates and manos were used for small, hard seeds, the mortar and pestle were used for larger, pulpier seeds, particularly acorns. It would seem, then, that acorns, or perhaps other large, pulpy seeds or nuts, became an important food resource beginning about 5000 B.P., although the continued prevalence of metates and manos indicates that small seeds remained valuable food resources. From this time on, however, the use of the metate and mano decreased in favor of the mortar and pestle, implying that acorns became increasingly important relative to small seeds.

Although acorns are practically a limitless food resource in many parts of California, the Channel region included, processing acorns into an edible food product is very time-consuming. Acorns contain tannic acid, which must be leached from the acorn meal through an elaborate procedure entailing placing the meal in a carefully prepared basin of damp sand near a creek or spring and gently pouring water over the meal. Because processing acorns is time- and labor-intensive, archaeologists have argued that acorns would not have been adopted as a food resource unless other comparable food resources could no longer support the regional population (Basgall 1987). Like seeds of grasses and annuals, acorns can be stored over the long term, which probably was the reason why they eventually became an important food product. At about 5000 B.P. acorns or other large seeds and nuts compensated for short-falls in the availability of small seeds.

Other than the introduction of the mortar and pestle and the subsistence change it implies, there is little evidence of cultural change. Interestingly, projectile points became more prevalent after about 5000 B.P. The points in use at this time were large side-notched or corner-notched points (Figure 2.3), which probably tipped darts (short, lightweight spears) propelled with the *atlatl* (throwing stick). However, the moderate abundances of animal bone refuse in middens of this age implies that hunting was no more important than previously, so the significance of the increased prevalence of projectile points is currently a mystery.

Sometime around 4500 B.P. another increase in population density appears to have occurred. During the following 1,500 years the importance of acorns and perhaps also marine fish and mammals may have increased, although evidence indicating these changes in subsistence is still scanty. Beginning 3000 B.P.–2500 B.P., however, the rate of cultural change appears to have accelerated. Sites serving as residential bases generally contain much denser midden refuse than before, often giving the soil matrix a sooty character. This may indicate that these residential bases were occupied for longer periods of time during an annual cycle. Bones of marine mammals and fish are often in relatively high densities in site deposits, implying that fishing and sea mammal hunting were becoming more important. The dart and atlatl continued to be used in hunting, but projectile points now had a contracting stem serving as the haft portion of the point (Figure 2.3).

Chester King has argued that social organization underwent a radical change sometime around 3000 B.P. On the basis of his analysis of mortuary practices, he feels that high-status positions in the society became hereditary at this time, and that high-status individuals accumulated wealth and controlled the exchange economy through ritual validation. However, Jeanne Arnold (1991:954–955, 1992a:68) has challenged this interpretation of the mortuary data. She believes that hereditary status, and other aspects of social and political complexity, did not evolve until quite late in prehistory, perhaps as late as 700 B.P. The problem is that King's interpretation of the timing of this event is based largely on data from only one cemetery, which is not a very large sample for inferring a region-wide cultural development. At least it can be said that status differentiation became more pronounced by about 2500 B.P., regardless of the criteria by which individuals came to occupy particular status positions.

The period between about 2500 B.P. and 800 B.P. appears to be one of steadily increasing importance of fishing and sea mammal hunting as subsistence pursuits, although the reality probably was more complicated than this. Nonetheless, an increasing diversity of fish species is represented in fish remains from sites of this period, undoubtedly in part the result of the introduction of the single-piece shell (sometimes bone) fishhook around 2500 B.P. (King 1990:83; Figure 2.3). Near the end of the period the harpoon was in use, indicated archaeologically by the presence of distinctive bone barbs known from ethnographic examples to be attached to the side of harpoon foreshafts (King 1990:85, 233; Figure 2.3). King (1990:85) argues that the harpoon had to be used with substantial watercraft, and he believes that the first evidence for the use of the plank canoe dates to the same time that harpoon parts first enter the archaeological record. Significantly, the plank canoe also would have facilitated cross-channel commerce.

Metates and manos are extremely rare in coastal sites of this time period, and mortars were increasingly more carefully shaped. Acorns probably became as important a food resource as they were at the time of European contact. As well, by the end of the period the bow and arrow had largely replaced the atlatl and dart, as reflected by the introduction of small leaf-shaped points.

Around 800 B.P. a new type of shell bead began to be made. The shell for this bead type came from the inner whorl, or callus, of the olivella shell (Figure 2.3). Mentioned earlier was the use by the Chumash of strings of this particular bead type as currency, so it would seem that the Chumash monetary exchange system documented ethnohistorically and ethnographically originated about 800 B.P. There is some disagreement among archaeologists, however, regarding whether the olivella callus bead was made this early. In her research on Santa Cruz Island, Arnold (1992b:137) found little evidence that olivella callus beads were used prevalently prior to around 700 B.P.

It will be remembered that Arnold argued against King's position that hereditary high-status positions became part of social organization by 2500 B.P. She proposed instead that this event occurred much later, between about 800 B.P. and 700 B.P. In fact, she argues that the development of the monetary system was facilitated by individuals who gained status and wealth by manipulating the cross-channel exchange system. Furthermore, she believes that 100 to 150 years prior to 700 B.P. was a period of subsistence stress induced by a period of warm and probably arid weather, and that the development of the monetary exchange system was a response to this period of stress (Arnold 1991, 1992a, 1992b). At any rate, at least by 700 B.P. olivella callus money was in use, and sites throughout the channel region dating after this time usually contain many times more olivella beads of all types than sites dating to earlier times.

The major change in subsistence occurring sometime around 800 B.P. was a marked increase in the importance of fishing. While other subsistence pursuits such as sea mammal hunting and shellfish collecting continued, their importance decreased relative to fishing. In addition to hook-and-line and harpoon, it is clear from the species represented among fish remains that various kinds of nets were used to obtain relatively small fish.

In conclusion, the type of cultural system that existed along the Santa Barbara Channel at the time of European contact came into existence by about 700 B.P. No obvious changes appear to have occurred after this date until Spanish colonization began in the 1770s and 1780s.

This overview of Santa Barbara Channel prehistory reveals that cultural systems became increasingly more complex within all realms of culture that are archaeologically visible. Subsistence practices entailed an expansion of the number of species of plants and animals exploited, and concomitantly subsistence technology became more elaborate. Social organization was largely egalitarian at the beginning but eventually involved status ranking and hereditary leadership. Finally, the economic system appears to have entailed increasing commerce between villages, eventually facilitated by the use of shell-bead money. It is important to recognize, however, that many of the details of cultural development have yet to be worked out, and some of the statements made in my overview surely will be revised in light of new data or new analyses of existing data.

Beyond the Santa Barbara Channel, a substantial amount of archaeology has been accomplished in the eastern portion of Chumash territory, both along the coast and in the inland valleys beyond the first range of mountains from the coast. Although a regional sequence is still quite hazy, it is clear that this region was occupied at least by 7000 B.P., and it is likely that the region saw continuous occupation into the historic period. Historically documented Chumash villages are scattered throughout this area, and some sites dating to earlier periods also appear to be main residential bases. Expectably, subsistence of populations living in interior valleys appears to have been oriented much more toward terrestrial resources, but the presence of shellfish remains and bones of fish and sea mammals indicate that food resources were imported from the nearby coast.

Some particularly definitive investigations were undertaken at Diablo Canyon in the northwestern sector of Chumash territory, where the Obispeño Chumash lived at the time of European contact. Greenwood (1972) carried out excavations at several coastal sites here, each containing midden deposits spanning relatively long segments of prehistory. The basal deposits at one site dated about 9000 B.P., which, at the time Greenwood's report was published in 1972, attracted considerable attention among California archaeologists. This basal stratum of deposits yielded shellfish remains and bones of fish that could be caught by hand in the intertidal zone (Fitch in Greenwood 1972). Even at this early time the sea was a significant source of food. No milling implements were present, and the very few projectile points from this stratum probably are from later occupation of the same site. The stratum directly above the 9,000-year-old deposits contained metates and manos. Deposits at a nearby site also containing metates and manos were dated as early as about 8500 B.P.

In general, the sequence of artifact types represented in the Diablo Canyon collections conforms to that of the Santa Barbara Channel, but the faunal remains revealed that shellfish generally were more important to the diet through the course of prehistory than was the case in the channel region. Conversely, a heavy dependence on fish and sea mammals appears never to have developed in the Diablo Canyon vicinity, although shore fishing and sea mammal hunting did take place.

Following Greenwood's report of dates around 9000 B.P. from one of the Diablo Canyon sites, archaeologists have discovered several other coastal sites in the region with dates in excess of 8000 B.P., indicating that there was a well-established population in the northwestern extreme of Chumash territory between 8000 B.P. and 9000 B.P. As we shall see, occupation in the Vandenberg region follows suit.

CONCLUSIONS

Archaeological research in the Santa Barbara Channel region has documented an evolution of culture from generalized hunter-gatherers to the maritime chiefdoms encountered by the Spanish expeditioners and colonists. Throughout the long prehistory of this region, populations were relatively sedentary, although less so earlier than later. Because archaeologists working in this region can view the increasing cultural complexity in technological, economic, and social realms, there are great opportunities for understanding how cultural evolution actually works.

Despite all the attractions offered by the archaeology of the Santa Barbara Channel region, other parts of the territory occupied by Chumash-speaking peoples also offer archaeologists some interesting research problems. Why, for instance, did occupation on the Channel Islands begin seemingly as early as it did on the mainland coast? How did occupations in the interior areas of Chumash territory, that is, up the major river valleys and beyond the first range of mountains from the coast, relate to the coastal regions? Regarding the Vandenberg region, how did the nearshore marine environment north of Point Conception affect cultural development in comparison to the much more benign Santa Barbara Channel? As we learn more about the archaeology of the less-studied portions of Chumash territory, we will find that comparative differences and similarities will serve as rich fodder for endeavors aimed at understanding the cultural variability of hunter-gatherer adaptations.

3

Research Background

THE LEGAL MANDATE FOR THE SHUTTLE PROJECT

When I first visited South Vandenberg in the early 1970s, I traveled along a two-lane highway that had been built in the mid-1960s to provide access to a large space launch complex. Construction of this highway resulted in the destruction of major portions of several archaeological sites. However, no archaeological investigations preceded the destruction of these archaeological resources, so we have no record of what was lost. Why, then, did the Air Force feel obliged a decade later to fund archaeological excavations at three of these sites at which further damage was anticipated due to the construction of the shuttlecraft tow route? The answer lies in changes to federal historic-preservation legislation during the intervening years.

The federal government had been involved in excavating sites affected by federally funded land development projects since the 1930s, when the Works Progress Administration collaborated with the Smithsonian Institution in employing archaeologists and legions of mostly unskilled laborers to carry out massive excavations, particularly of sites that would be inundated or otherwise destroyed by construction of dams along rivers. After the Second World War, archaeology in response to dam construction continued on a more moderate scale. Eventually, these archaeological projects came under the administration of the National Park Service, and in 1960 they became legally mandated by the Reservoir Salvage Act. Although federal funds were made available to carry out the excavations of sites affected by dam construction and inundation, very little of these funds were allocated to analysis of the resulting data and preparation of reports. Salvage archaeology, as this kind of archaeology came to be called, meant simply the retrieval of artifacts and other site information before the sites were destroyed or inundated, and many collections still sit unanalyzed in museums and other collections repositories (see King et al. 1977 for a history of federally funded archaeological programs).

The context of salvage archaeology began to change with the passage in 1966 of the National Historic Preservation Act (amended extensively in 1992). This act established the National Register of Historic Places, which was meant to include not only buildings and other kinds of structures of historical significance but also archaeological sites deemed to be significant because of their potential to contribute to knowledge of prehistory or history and more generally to the discipline of archaeology. Section 106 of the act was particularly crucial to the development of a more responsible consideration of archaeological sites endangered by construction projects.

This section required federal agencies planning a land development project of any sort—not just dams—to consider whether the project might affect archaeological sites listed on the National Register, and to consult with the newly formed Advisory Council on Historic Preservation if a listed archaeological site might be affected.

The problem, however, was that a site already had to be listed on the National Register before any consideration was given to it, and of course very few were. Federal agencies were not obliged to find out whether still-unrecorded sites were present in a project area and, if so, whether any qualified for inclusion on the National Register. It was not until 1976 that revisions to the act were passed that, in essence, required federal agencies to perform surveys as part of their project planning to determine whether archaeological sites eligible for inclusion on the National Register were present. In the meantime, however, President Nixon in 1971 issued Executive Order 11593, which directed landholding federal agencies to inventory all of their properties and to nominate to the National Register potentially eligible archaeological sites. The order also specified that federal agencies should proceed cautiously with land development plans until such an inventory could be completed. This executive order accomplished much of what the 1976 revisions to the National Historic Preservation Act eventually put into law.

Another important piece of legislation passed around this time was the National Environmental Policy Act of 1969. This act required federal agencies to prepare an "environmental impact statement" for any development project that might adversely affect the environment. The concept of "environment" in this act is quite broad, including not only natural resources but also historic and archaeological resources. Federal agencies responsive to the various intents of this act recognized the need to perform surveys for archaeological sites as part of an assessment of potential environmental impacts. However, this act did not go so far as to require explicitly that such surveys be performed.

In 1974 the Archaeological and Historic Preservation Act was signed into law. This law amended the Reservoir Salvage Act of 1960 by requiring federal agencies to preserve significant archaeological data that would be destroyed by any federal land development project. Although the title of this law implies that it would have had profound impact on procedures for preserving of archaeological resources, its main benefit was simply to reinforce the obligations of federal agencies when archaeological sites had to be destroyed as a result of development projects. In this regard, the law authorizes federal agencies to expend up to 1 percent of the project costs to recover and analyze archaeological data that otherwise would be lost. It was the combination of the National Historic Preservation Act of 1966 (with its 1976 revisions) and the National Environmental Policy Act of 1969 that began to induce federal agencies to consider avoiding destruction of significant archaeological sites when planning development projects, even if the locations of the sites were not yet known; and if avoidance of destructive impacts was not possible, to implement a data recovery program to mitigate these impacts.

Brief mention should be made of the Archaeological Resources Protection Act, signed into law in 1979. This law expands the scope of the Antiquities Act of 1906 by affording greater protection to archaeological sites on federal property from unauthorized collecting activities, informally referred to as looting and pothunting. It also addresses flaws in the 1906 act exposed by legal challenges. Since the 1979 act was passed, a number of illegal collectors have been arrested, tried, and given stiff fines or even jail sentences.

By themselves, the laws are relatively general in their wording. Typical of such federal laws, appropriate federal agencies had to write implementing regulations soon after the laws were passed. After considerable review and revision, including input from many archaeologists, the regulations implementing these laws were published in the Federal Register and integrated into the Code of Federal Regulations. One of the most important sets of regulations is known as 36 CFR 800 (Code of Federal Regulations, Title 36, Part 800). Issued by the Advisory Council on Historic Preservation, these regulations provide guidance to federal agencies attempting to comply with Section 106 of the National Historic Preservation Act. In addition to regulations, a number of guidelines have been issued by those federal offices responsible for the nation's historic preservation program (mainly in the Department of Interior). For instance, The Advisory Council on Historic Preservation published a guide to compliance with 36 CFR 800 titled *Treatment of Archaeological Properties: A Handbook.*

The Shuttle Project began during the early years of the development of an effective archaeological resources preservation program mandated by the National Historic Preservation Act, the National Environmental Policy Act, and Executive Order 11593. In fact, the 1974 survey and evaluation of sites, the project's first phase of work, was not yet formally required by law. The Air Force realized, however, in light of advice from federal archaeologists connected with the Interagency Archaeological Services (a division of the National Park Service), that survey and site evaluation would be a prudent way to obtain information on the nature of archaeological resources in order to comply with the two laws and the executive order.

SHUTTLE PROJECT HISTORY

In terms of the logic set forth in the historic preservation legislation just discussed, the first step was to determine the location of archaeological sites in the corridor of land where space shuttle facilities might be built. In the early stages of their planning, the Air Force did not know exactly where they wanted to place their facilities. Indeed, they realized that locations of environmentally sensitive areas, such as the locations of particularly significant archaeological sites or patches of endangered plant species, required them to be flexible in deciding where facilities ultimately would be constructed. For this reason, the corridor of land that became the subject of the survey and site evaluation phase of the Shuttle Project was relatively large, extending along approximately 32 km of South Vandenberg coastline and 3,000 feet (914 m) inland from the coast (Figure 3.1). Information on significant natural and archaeological resources in this relatively large corridor allowed them maneuvering room, so to speak, in placing the space shuttle facilities.

Because one of UCSB's graduate students, Larry Spanne, had carried out an extensive archaeological survey on the base in the early 1970s, and because of my involvement in Santa Barbara Channel archaeology, UCSB was the logical place to

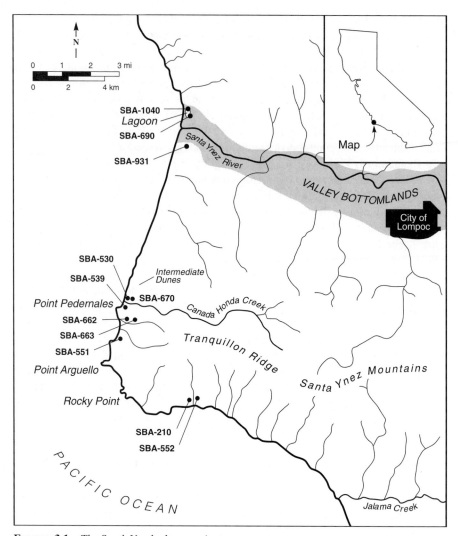

FIGURE 3.1   *The South Vandenberg project area.*

come for archaeological expertise. The Air Force provided funds to the Interagency Archaeological Services' regional office in San Francisco for the sites' survey and assessment, and in turn the Interagency Archaeological Services contracted UCSB to do the work. At that time, Vandenberg Air Force Base did not have an archaeologist on its staff, so it made sense to place contract administration responsibilities in the hands of federal archaeologists in the Interagency Archaeological Services.

By 1973, 41 sites were known to exist within the 3,000-foot-wide land corridor on South Vandenberg, so the Air Force recognized from the start that archaeological resources had to be considered in their planning. Very little was known about these sites, however, and we were not sure that all sites in the land corridor had been located. As a consequence, a main objective of the 1974 phase of investigations was to perform a thorough survey of all lands in the land corridor and record all sites located, no matter how small or ephemeral. We located and recorded 39 new sites in the land corridor, bringing the total to 80.

Because so little was known about sites in the land corridor, and for that matter in the region in general, the other main objective of the 1974 investigations was to undertake test excavations to collect enough data to determine whether any of the sites met criteria for nomination to the National Register of Historic Places. The information from test excavations also allowed us to estimate the financial cost of excavations at each site should destructive impacts be unavoidable once the Air Force had completed the construction planning.

We carried out the fieldwork during the summer months in 1974 by a team consisting of a field director (Larry Spanne), two excavation crew chiefs, a survey crew chief, a field laboratory crew chief, and between 20 and 35 crew members. One of our crew members was of Chumash Indian descent; she, along with four other Chumash descendants, served as advisors to our project on matters of concern to the local Chumash community, including the Chumash living in the vicinity of the city of Santa Barbara and on the Santa Ynez Indian Reservation located 47 km east of Vandenberg.

As survey and test excavations progressed, it became obvious that the land corridor contained many more sites, some containing large volumes of relatively deep cultural deposits, than could be tested with the available time and money. As mentioned in Chapter 1, two of the sites quite unexpectedly turned out to be more than five meters deep, apparently over areas of a few acres. Large amounts of field time were consumed in excavating just a few test units in these two sites, thus seriously affecting our schedule of fieldwork. To compensate for this unanticipated complexity of the archaeological record in the land corridor, our work plan was revised so as to include in the testing program only those sites that stood the greatest chance of being affected by space shuttle facilities construction. In the end, we were able to perform some level of test excavation at 31 sites, all of which were near alternative routes where a shuttlecraft tow route might be constructed or near a large, unused launch complex that probably would be remodeled for the space shuttle.

My field director and I submitted a preliminary report to the Interagency Archaeological Services and the Air Force shortly after fieldwork was completed, and we completed the final report in 1976 (Glassow et al. 1976). The final report was focused on evaluation of the significance of the sites and included only enough analysis of the data for that purpose. Funds were not available for a thorough analysis of the relatively large volume of data that we had collected. This was quite disheartening to us, for we realized that the body of data had considerable potential for telling us something about the prehistory of the region. Once the Interagency Archaeological Services and the Air Force accepted our final report (not without some revisions in response to comments on the initial draft), our obligations under the contract were completed.

Once the Air Force had completed the basic aspects of its planning in 1977, it was apparent that three sites would be affected by widening of road cuts along the existing highway through South Vandenberg to the space shuttle launch complex. This highway was to serve as the route along which the shuttlecraft would be towed to the launch complex, and the road cuts had to be widened to accommodate its wingspread. All three sites had been tested in 1974, and interestingly the radiocarbon dates obtained at that time indicated that their prehistoric occupations were dispersed through nearly 8,000 years of prehistory.

The Air Force again called on the Interagency Archaeological Services to administer a contract for excavations at these three sites, analysis of the resulting data, and report preparation. Interagency Archaeological Services sent requests for proposals for this work to a number of archaeologists working in California, including myself. My proposal was accepted, and I then began the task of putting together another large project.

The contract between UCSB and the National Park Service (representing the Air Force) was signed in October 1978. We began fieldwork a few weeks later and worked through the spring of the following year. Excavations were restricted to strips of land one to three meters wide adjacent to existing road cuts through the three sites. Upon completion of our excavations, these strips of land were to be removed to widen the road cuts.

I served as principal investigator, and I was assisted by a co-principal investigator, Pandora Snethkamp, who was director of UCSB's Office of Public Archaeology. As was the case with the 1974 project, we maintained a field laboratory in an unused building on South Vandenberg. The crew lived in barracks located on North Vandenberg while fieldwork was in progress. The organization of the crew was somewhat more complex than that used in 1974. There was a field director and two crew chiefs, a mapping crew chief, a field photographer, and a laboratory director and two laboratory crew chiefs. The project employed 21 field and laboratory workers through most of the fieldwork. Four of the crew members were Native American trainees, and a member of the Santa Ynez Indian Reservation served as a field monitor and advisor to the project.

The main portion of the fieldwork was completed in August 1979. However, due to slight realignments to the tow route right-of-way, additional work had to be done at two of the sites. This work was undertaken in February 1980, and shortly thereafter several field crew members monitored removal of the remaining road cut deposits that we did not excavate.

The funding for the data analysis and report preparation was separated from that for the fieldwork. We completed a preliminary report in 1981, which included a basic description of the fieldwork and the artifact collections (Glassow et al. 1981). This report also included an outline of a research design for the data analysis based on what we knew at that point about the data we had obtained from the three sites. Before we could obtain the funding for the data analysis and report preparation, we had to write a proposal for these activities that was acceptable to the Interagency Archaeological Services. For a variety of reasons, the funding did not become available until near the end of 1985, and when it did, the amount was a good deal less than had been allocated when the contract began in 1978.

When full-scale analysis began in late 1985, essentially all of the collections from the three sites had been cataloged. These catalogs existed as three computer data files. Much of the collections analysis entailed developing a more refined artifact typology than that used during the cataloging in the field laboratory. As well, a good deal of effort was devoted to taxonomic identification of mammal, bird, and fish bones and to an analysis of the flaked stone collections, including waste flakes.

energy possible (assuming a more-or-less constant rate of energy expenditure) for a given amount of time devoted to subsistence pursuits. To accomplish this goal, they exploit only certain potential food resources out of the typically wide array available in their environment. The particular combination of food resources actually exploited is the *optimal diet*. The definition of an optimal diet, however, ideally should consider whether *time* devoted to acquiring a particular food resource or the *quantity* of the food resource is of most value. If the food resource is consumed quickly after it is acquired, a group of hunter-gatherers will try to minimize the amount of time expended to meet immediate dietary needs. Conversely, if the food resource is stored, a group will try to maximize the quantity acquired and will not be as concerned with time expended.

In predicting what an optimal diet would be in a given environmental situation, potential food resources are ranked according to the rate at which food energy is acquired for a given amount of time and energy expended. The measurement of the rate of food energy acquisition is made at the time that a food resource is encountered, and it specifically does not take into consideration time and effort devoted to searching for the food resource. According to optimal foraging theory, a given food resource is included in the optimal diet so long as its food energy return per unit of time and effort devoted to obtaining and processing this food resource is greater than the food energy return per unit of time and effort devoted to obtaining, processing, *and* searching for of all the more highly ranked food resources. In other words, the greater the scarcity of highly ranked food resources already included in the diet, which translates into longer search times necessary to encounter these resources, the greater the likelihood that the next lower-ranked resource will become economical to exploit. The number of food resources actually exploited is called the *diet breadth*.

Paradoxically, it is possible that the highest-ranked food resource actually does not contribute the greatest proportion of the total food energy consumed by a population. For instance, deer often are the highest-ranked food resource in western North American environments, but their low abundance or the considerable time expended in searching for them during a hunt may be such that they could provide only a small proportion of the human population's needed food energy. A lower-ranked resource such as jackrabbits might be so abundant (and prolific) that they are able to supply the greater bulk of the food energy needs. Such a situation on the face of it seems counterintuitive, and indeed one could argue that deer might be so rare that the time expended in searching for the few available would not be worth the effort. Still, if the rare deer fortuitously were encountered while hunting for rabbits or other game animals, more than likely a hunter would take advantage of the opportunity because of the substantial return in food energy for the amount of effort he would expend in killing the animal. Regardless of its rarity, the deer in this example would remain in the optimal diet.

It should be relatively obvious that changing human population density or changing environmental conditions may affect diet breadth. For example, if population density increases, more demand is placed on food resources already exploited, and some are likely to become increasingly costly to exploit because search time increases as the resources become rarer. As search time for highly ranked food resources already in the diet increases, a point eventually will be reached when a resource ranked just below those already in the diet becomes economical to exploit. In short, diet breadth increases as human population increases in an otherwise stable environment. The same result would occur if environmental degradation caused food resources in the diet to become scarcer, independent of human exploitation. Here again, search time would increase, and therefore lower-ranked food resources are added to the diet. In contrast to these scenarios, if population density were to decrease in a stable environment, or if food resources became more productive due, say, to a climatic change, then we would expect diet breadth to become narrower as lower-ranked food resources no longer are exploited.

The relationship between the two problem areas that guided my research now should be clear. The role of shellfish in a prehistoric diet may be viewed from the perspective of optimal foraging theory by considering how shellfish would have ranked in relationship to other food resources, such as various species of land and sea mammals, nearshore fish, marine birds, and various plant foods, such as acorns and hard seeds. In light of arguments made by Alan Osborn (1977), shellfish should rank very low and should not be included in the diet unless a wide variety of more highly ranked food resources are scarce. However, as I have just argued, scarcity (or abundance) is dependent on both the size of human population of a region and environmental conditions. With regard to the Vandenberg region, we would expect that human population density was sufficiently high, or that environmental conditions created sufficient scarcity of highly ranked food resources, that the prehistoric diet was so broad as to include shellfish. Moreover, we would expect the importance of shellfish to fluctuate as the abundance of more highly ranked food resources fluctuated, assuming that population density was stable.

Aside from changes in population and environment on subsistence change, I considered the possibility that population density and environmental fluctuations were directly related to each other. Specifically, it seemed reasonable to hypothesize that a decrease in the productivity of food resources may have resulted in a decrease in population density. Expansion of diet breadth in the face of lowered productivity of already exploited food resources may not always have been possible, especially if the decrease in productivity affected most food resources quite severely. My thinking along these lines was prompted by studies of the health of prehistoric populations of the American Southwest, which in turn rely on studies of health among subsistence farmers of the modern era (Wetterstrom 1986:111–123; Martin et al. 1991:207–222). Assuming that expansion of diet breadth was not an adequate solution to declining food resource productivity, some degree of malnourishment would occur. Malnourishment has a relatively rapid effect on population by increasing mortality among infants, children, and the elderly and by reducing the rate of reproduction. Under such conditions regional population numbers would have declined significantly within only one or two generations and would have remained low until environmental conditions improved or other means of acquiring food resources were adopted.

I should not neglect to mention the effects of technological change on subsistence systems. One might argue, for instance, that the introduction of new fishing technology may have served to increase the rate at which fish could be acquired, which in turn would have allowed larger numbers of people to be supported. This is true, of course, but new technology of this sort is not without its costs in the form of increases in labor devoted to manufacturing and maintaining the new technological items. Furthermore, manufacture and use of new technology requires reallocation of both labor and time, that is, changes in other aspects of a cultural system. For that matter, if population numbers declined relatively rapidly at the onset of a period of subsistence stress, there would be little incentive to develop or adopt new technology because the decline would have relieved much of the stress. I suspect that integration of new technology into a cultural system always was difficult and would not occur unless a population was experiencing persistent and severe subsistence stress. In other words, persistent and severe subsistence stress would have created strong incentives to increase diet breadth. Technological change would be expected to occur when adverse environmental conditions had caused regional population density to decline to relatively low levels. Once new subsistence technology was integrated into a cultural system, however, population numbers potentially could rise to significantly higher levels once the period of subsistence stress had ended.

There are other aspects of cultural change, in addition to subsistence change, that could be of concern to archaeologists working in the Vandenberg region. I mentioned in Chapter 2 the development of regional economic exchange systems that occurred during Santa Barbara Channel prehistory. In considering how the populations of the Vandenberg region articulated with this development, it makes sense to ask first what kinds of products did the Vandenberg region contribute to the exchange system. We know that Vandenberg sites dating to the late prehistoric period contain the same types of shell beads that served as money among the Chumash living along the Santa Barbara Channel, which implies that the economic system of the Channel region included the Vandenberg region. But what could the people living in the Vandenberg region provide that would be in demand by the Channel dwellers? One possibility is suggested by the considerable abundance of chert-flaking debris in many Vandenberg sites. It is possible that Vandenberg populations produced for trade chert projectile points and knives, or perhaps preforms from which these bifaces could be manufactured. Chert available along the Santa Barbara Channel is of low quality, whereas that in the Vandenberg region is of much better quality and considerably more abundant. Therefore, it is reasonable to hypothesize that Vandenberg populations specialized to some extent in chert biface manufacture in order to acquire through exchange various products from the Santa Barbara Channel, including shell-bead money.

The development of the interregional exchange networks might be linked to fluctuations in population density or environment. I mentioned in Chapter 2 Arnold's proposal that intensive use of shell beads apparently beginning slightly before 700 B.P. was a result of a climatic interval during which the nearshore marine environment was degraded. Arnold argued that this environmental change favored increased regional exchange and the use of shell-bead money. However, such climatic fluctuations certainly occurred earlier in prehistory; indeed, paleoclimatic data indicate that some were more severe than the one ending about 700 B.P. Why did a monetized economy not develop during one of these earlier climatic events? I suspect that part of the answer to this question lies in the lower population densities that existed at these times. If population density increased significantly by late prehistoric times, intensification of exchange may have been the most efficient way to support increasingly more people in a region with stable or even declining amounts of food resources. In earlier times, when population densities presumably were lower, regional exchange may have been more difficult to intensify. In other words, when population density became relatively high, the flow of food resources between different villages in an exchange network may have been a more viable alternative than expanding diet breadth.

A research design is, of course, more than a presentation of theoretical arguments and a series of hypotheses derived from them. Equally important is the specification of the various kinds of data that will be necessary for evaluating the hypotheses and, as necessary, the bridging arguments that link data to the variables that a hypothesis proposes are related. The kinds of data one needs to collect then allows specification of the manner in which excavations, collections processing, and ultimately data analysis are to be carried out.

At the time I first was developing my research design for my Vandenberg excavations, I had no good information for conceiving specific hypotheses about the determinants of subsistence change based on the tenets of optimal foraging theory. In fact, I had no idea what the subsistence changes might have been, although earlier excavations at least had identified a number of food resources that were dietarily important through most of prehistory. Furthermore, although I had access to paleoenvironmental data derived from sediment cores obtained by oceanographers from the bottom of the Santa Barbara Channel, these data were not sufficient for inferring much about changes in the abundances of different kinds of food resources. I suspected that human population density had fluctuated through time and that there probably was a trend toward increasing density through time, but I had not conceived of any good measure of populational change.

Even though I did not have enough information for developing specific hypotheses about subsistence change, economic principles such as those of optimal foraging theory did provide a basis for deciding what kinds of data I should collect if I was to have any chance of studying subsistence change and its determinants, and it forced me to consider how I might devise different measures of such variables as changes in population density.

For that matter, a rigorous application of optimal foraging theory to archaeological situations requires a good deal of quantitative information on the distribution, abundance, and behavior of potential food resources that a prehistoric population might have exploited, as well as the time and energy consumed in using specific technologies to acquire and process each of the potential food resources. Of course, archaeologists typically have access to only bits and pieces of this kind of information, so the application of optimal foraging theory to archaeological situations requires much rougher kinds of measurement of these variables than would be possible in ethnographic studies of contemporary peoples.

Information on subsistence practices could be derived from two forms of archaeological data: food remains and artifacts used to acquire and process food resources. The best-preserved food remains in Vandenberg sites are marine shells and bones of sea and land mammals, fish, and birds. Carbonized seeds are found in some sites, but preservation appears to be quite variable. Subsistence-related artifacts include milling equipment, projectile points, and fishhooks. I also was concerned with obtaining evidence of the nature and intensity of economic exchange. Shell beads were an obvious indicator of exchange, particularly if there was little or no evidence of manufacture of shell beads in Vandenberg sites, that is, small fragments of olivella shells that were the waste from bead making as well as the chert microdrills for perforating the beads. To determine whether projectile points and knives were being manufactured beyond the needs of the Vandenberg populations, abundance of chert waste flakes and preforms indicative of particular stages of biface manufacture had to be assessed.

I had hoped to obtain paleoenvironmental information from fossil pollen preserved in the site deposits and in sediments of intermittent ponds that had formed behind coastal dunes. George Batchelder, a professional palynologist, was commissioned to undertake an exploratory study to determine the potential of palynological data. Unfortunately, fossil pollen was poorly preserved in site deposits, and there was the additional problem of mixing caused by rodent burrowing. A soil core taken from the more promising of the intermittent ponds did yield fossil pollen, but small quantities. Although I wished to pursue this research further, federal archaeologists at the Interagency Archaeological Services did not feel the results were definitive enough to justify doing so. In lieu of palynology, I anticipated that a study of soils and geomorphology of the sites and their vicinities would provide some paleoenvironmental information even though the focus of this study was on the depositional histories of the sites.

Measurement of human population density has always been an extremely difficult task for archaeologists. Indeed, it is particularly difficult among prehistoric hunter-gatherers, who typically occupy a number of different sites during a given year and from one year to the next. At the time I prepared the first version of the research design, I had no idea how to go about measuring population numbers, but by the time I was involved in the data analysis, I had struck upon a means of obtaining a rough idea of relative changes in regional population. The approach I developed was to tabulate frequencies of all radiocarbon dates from the whole Vandenberg region per 200-year interval. A published listing of California radiocarbon dates organized by county (Breschini et al. 1992) made this task relatively easy, although I had to determine which dates in the Santa Barbara County list pertained to Vandenberg sites. In cases where a site was associated with two or more radiocarbon dates separated by less than 200 years, the dates were grouped by approximate 200-year intervals, and an average of each group was counted as one date. This procedure compensated for the fact that some sites were associated with many more radiocarbon dates than others.

Consistent with an argument developed by John Rick (1987), my reasoning for using frequencies of radiocarbon dates per time interval as a measure of changes in population density is as follows: (1) the 54 archaeological sites in the Vandenberg region for which radiocarbon dates existed at the time of my study are a roughly representative sample of the region's archaeological deposits; (2) variations in frequencies of dates per 200-year interval therefore reflects variations in the total volume of deposits per 200-year interval in the region; (3) the greater the regional population, the larger the volume of deposits will be created in a region; and (4) consequently, the frequency of dates in a 200-year interval should be the approximate result of the number of people living during that interval. This logic admittedly may be assailed, but it gains some credibility by the fact that lists of radiocarbon dates for neighboring regions and elsewhere in California exhibit similar patterns of variation, even though there are differences, too. This implies that some of the factors causing fluctuations in frequencies of radiocarbon dates are common to large areas of California. I will consider some of these common patterns in Chapter 6.

The final element of the research design to be discussed is data collection and processing procedures. As I mentioned earlier, excavations beginning in the fall of 1978 took place at three sites along strips of land adjacent to existing road cuts. At two of these sites, SBA-539 and 931, these strips of land, which I shall call impact areas hereafter, passed through the central portion of the deposits. As a consequence, the impact areas could be treated as linear transects through the center of these sites. Distributing units along a transect of this sort is a reasonable way to obtain a representative sample from coastal sites of the sort found in the Vandenberg region, although having access to the whole site area certainly would be more ideal. The impact area at the third site, SBA-670, passed through one edge, where cultural remains were in relatively low densities. We were to discover during excavation, however, that another deeply buried midden existed near the base of the road cut, and it appeared that the impact area passed through the approximate center of this midden stratum.

I knew the project budget would not allow complete excavation of each impact area. For that matter, complete excavation would have yielded much larger collections than were needed for addressing most research problems. Consequently, I devised a sampling design in which the length of each impact area was divided into 1 m intervals. The initial phase of the fieldwork entailed excavation of a 5 percent sample, so the 1 m intervals were divided into groups of 20, and one from each group was selected by reference to a random numbers table. For purposes of excavation, each strip of land defined by a 1 m interval was divided into 2 m segments, normally resulting in a row of two or more 1 m×2 m excavation units extending from the back edge of the impact area to the road cut (Figure 3.2). All units in each selected row were excavated as part of the 5 percent sample. Each 1 m×2 m unit was excavated in 10 cm levels.

The initial 5 percent sample gave us an idea of variations in densities of cultural remains along the lengths of the impact areas. This information allowed my field team and I to make a series of decisions regarding how to increase the sample size in ways that would maximize the information value of the data. At SBA-931 we decided to concentrate much of our effort in a 4 m×12 m area excavation where cultural remains were densest and where there was some possibility of discerning spatial distributions of point-provenienced artifacts. (Point-proveniencing entails plotting the areal location and measuring the depth from datum of each artifact.) At the other two sites we opted to increase the sample size by excavating additional randomly selected unit rows. We ultimately excavated between 13 and 25 percent of the different impact areas within site boundaries.

Excavation procedures had to be adjusted to the fact that many of the items of interest are quite small. I opted to sift large proportions of the excavated deposits through eighth-inch mesh screens in order to collect systematically such items as small fish vertebrae, small shell fragments, and fragments of fishhooks. As well, I

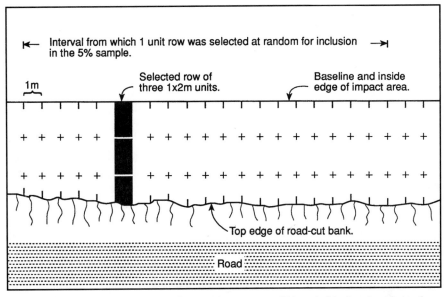

FIGURE 3.2 *A typical unit layout along an impact area. Although this drawing shows the intersections of all possible units within a section of an impact area, only the corners of those units to be excavated were defined by stakes in the field. Note that the unit intersecting the bank is incomplete, requiring that the volume of the unit be calculated from drawings of its lateral wall profiles.*

decided that finding small fragments of bone and rare fishhook fragments required cleaning and drying all the residues retained by the screens and then sorting the residues in the field laboratory where lighting could be controlled and the exigencies of excavation did not induce haste in sorting.

In order to recover samples of carbonized seeds and other small items of interest that would pass through the eighth-inch mesh screens, I decided to obtain *column samples* from selected excavation units. Column samples typically are excavated from the sidewalls of completed units. Ours were 25 cm×25 cm or 50 cm×50 cm in horizontal dimensions and were divided vertically into the same 10-cm levels used to excavate the adjacent unit. We collected all the soil from the columns without field screening, and at the field lab we used flotation to extract small, relatively light items, or the *light fraction,* from the soil from each level of each column. Our relatively simple technique of flotation entailed placing the soil from each column level into a bucket and then filling the bucket with water with a strong jet from a nozzle attached to a garden hose. While the water was still turbid, which kept small, relatively light items in suspension, it was poured through a screen with 40 meshes to the inch. The bucket was then refilled in the same manner and the procedure repeated until very few suspended items were being poured out. As a last step, the residues left in the bottom of the bucket, the *heavy fraction,* were washed through a sixteenth-inch mesh screen.

My objective was to use the power of the computer for purposes of data management and analysis. Consequently, my project colleagues and I developed a coding system for describing all categories of artifacts, faunal remains, and other items of interest. When I began the project in 1978, desktop computers were just becoming available, and software for them was still very limited. Consequently, our cataloging was done on coding forms, which later were inputted into mainframe computer files for access by the Statistical Analysis System (SAS), a statistical software package on one of UCSB's mainframe computers. Once I began my analysis in 1985, we decided to download the catalog files from the mainframe to a desktop computer so that we could work more conveniently and cheaply with the catalog data in the course of analysis. We made most use of dBase III-plus, Systat, and Reflex for data management and statistical compilation.

I mentioned earlier that some of the data collected in 1974 were included in the analysis in order to provide regional breadth to the analysis. However, because the 1974 excavations entailed more cursory collection procedures, particularly with regard to screening of deposits and sorting through residues retained by screens, the 1974 data were not always comparable to that from the later phase of the project. This lack of comparability was especially troublesome with regard to faunal remains. Many small fish bones and small fragments of sea mammal bone were not systematically recovered in 1974, whereas they were during the investigations beginning in 1978. As a consequence, analysis of faunal remains had to be divided into two aspects. One utilized collections retained by eighth-inch mesh screens and sorted from screen residues in a field laboratory. These collections came from the column samples collected in 1974 as well as many of the units excavated during the mitigation phase of the project. The other aspect utilized collections from the 1974 units that were obtained from quarter-inch mesh screens while units were being excavated.

In this brief description of the project research design I have omitted numerous details and minor changes that were made through the duration of the project. I also have not mentioned a number of glitches that were largely the result of my never before having directed a project of this size and complexity. The more significant of these research design details will become apparent as I describe the work at individual sites and the results of the data analysis.

4

Chronological Framework

INTRODUCTION

In the course of most archaeological projects a good deal of attention must be given to dating sites and developing a regional chronology. Prior to the Shuttle Project, very few sites in the Vandenberg region had yielded chronological information of any sort. As a consequence, there was no regional chronology to speak of, although my colleagues and I suspected that the Vandenberg region's chronology probably paralleled that of the neighboring Santa Barbara Channel. The principal means of determining when sites in the Vandenberg region were occupied has been *radiocarbon dating,* which is based on the constant rate of decay of the radioactive carbon isotope, ^{14}C, in the remains of once-living organisms. In the 1950s archaeologists working in California quickly embraced radiocarbon dating, and today it is fundamental to all efforts to determine the antiquity of site occupations. At the time I was analyzing data from the Shuttle Project in 1987, other archaeologists and I had obtained radiocarbon dates from 81 sites in the region; 45 of these were obtained in the context of the Shuttle Project, and the rest were obtained in the course of subsequent projects.

I used the presence or absence of time-sensitive artifact forms, particularly shell beads of distinctive types, as a supplement to radiocarbon dating. The times during prehistory when these artifact forms were in use had been established to a greater or lesser degree through previous research, primarily in the Santa Barbara Channel region. Knowing this, I was able to use the dates established for these artifacts to *cross-date* Vandenberg sites. Because this previous research entailed associating distinctive artifact forms with radiocarbon dates, all my efforts to assign absolute dates to sites depended ultimately on radiocarbon dating.

RADIOCARBON DATING

Constructing a chronology based on radiocarbon dates is not simply a matter of submitting samples of datable material such as charcoal or shell to a radiocarbon dating laboratory, receiving a date from the laboratory a month or so later, and listing the dates in chronological order. A number of factors must be considered when deriving chronological information from radiocarbon dates. Importantly, some of these factors determine the temporal resolution inferable from the depositional context of the radiocarbon date.

Seldom does one find in Vandenberg sites organic material for a radiocarbon date in a discrete, undisturbed depositional context such as a hearth or a floor level. The reason is that depositional distinctions have been blurred through agents of soil movement, by far the most common being the California pocket gopher (see discussion in Chapter 1). As a result of such disturbances, the spatial context of organic materials usable in radiocarbon dating no longer may be the same as when originally deposited. For example, a marine shell from which a radiocarbon date could be obtained may have dropped down a rodent burrow into a level that dates perhaps 200 years earlier than the date when the inhabitants of the site collected the shell and brought it to the site.

With regard to selection of organic material for radiocarbon dating, during excavations we generally collected samples such as a large lump or a cluster of small lumps of charcoal, a complete marine shell, or a pocket of shell fragments. While these contexts are seemingly discrete, their associations with other depositional phenomena usually were not clear. As well, when a sample consisted of a number of charcoal lumps or pieces of shell (sometimes several dozen), there is always the chance that it has been contaminated to some degree by rodent disturbance. Despite our care in selecting samples, some dates may represent the average age of two or more depositional events separated in time by as much as several hundred years.

Another problem in interpreting radiocarbon dates concerns specifically those dates derived from marine shell. A date derived from this type of organic material is subject to significant error due to what are known as *fractionation effects*. Depending on where a living organism obtains its carbonates (as food or through photosynthesis), the ratio of stable carbon isotopes, ^{13}C to ^{12}C, may vary. This ratio will affect the ratio of ^{14}C to ^{12}C, which is measured to obtain a radiocarbon date. As a result of fractionation effects, which I had the radiocarbon laboratory determine in the course of generating a date, I found that marine shell samples from Vandenberg sites were *too young* by 400 to 440 years. As a result, one should correct these dates by adding the number of years indicated by the results from the radiocarbon laboratory.

An additional source of error in the radiocarbon date itself is the *reservoir effect*. Again, it is dates from marine shell that are subject to this effect, but in this case the effect operates in the other direction by making the sample appear *too old*. Some of the carbonates consumed by a live shellfish are ultimately derived from organisms that lived in the ocean several hundred years earlier. The "old" carbon from these sources becomes part of the shell. Along the central California coast in the vicinity of Vandenberg, the reservoir effect makes samples appear approximately 625 years too old, and this amount therefore must be subtracted from the raw date. However, the reservoir effect probably varies somewhat from one location to another along the coast due to variations in ocean currents and intensity of local upwelling of sea waters. Unfortunately, the reservoir effect on a shell sample cannot be determined from its isotopic constituents as is the case with fractionation effects. Scientists determined the amount of the reservoir effect by dating shells collected at a known historical date prior to atmospheric contamination caused by detonation of atom bombs.

Of course, fractionation effects and the reservoir effect cancel each other to a large extent. While fractionation effects make a shell sample appear typically 430 years too young, the reservoir effect makes the same sample appear 625 years too old. Consequently, to correct a raw radiocarbon date from a marine shell sample, about 195 years must be subtracted from it. It is conventional to refer to such a date as a *corrected* date (see Taylor 1987:120–123, 126–132, for a discussion of fractionation and reservoir effects).

Radiocarbon dates derived from charcoal are not subject to such sources of significant error, although one must be reasonably confident that the charcoal in a prehistoric hearth was not already several hundred years old when collected as firewood by the site's inhabitants. I obtained some of the Shuttle Project's radiocarbon dates from charcoal samples, but because charcoal is only rarely found in large enough pieces or concentrations for a date, marine shell, which is generally very abundant in Vandenberg sites, was used for the larger proportion of the radiocarbon dates.

As I mentioned, variation in the reservoir effect still is poorly known; it may be more or less than the published correction of 625 years for the central California coast. Nonetheless, it seems reasonable to assume that the reservoir correction may be in the order of 625 years on the basis of pairs of dates from charcoal and shell samples collected from the same provenience. For instance, in the course of my work at Point Sal, just north of Vandenberg, a shell date of 960±60 B.P. and a charcoal date of 760±90 B.P were collected from the same 10-cm-thick stratum in a test unit (Glassow 1991). If we subtract 195 years from the shell date (625 years of reservoir effect minus 430 years of average fractionation effects), the two dates become nearly identical. For purposes of the analysis presented in Chapter 6, I "corrected" all raw radiocarbon dates derived from shell samples by subtracting 195 years from them so that they would be comparable to dates derived from charcoal.

One also must recognize a distinction between *radiocarbon years* and *calendar years*. Because the amount of the ^{14}C isotope available in the world's biosphere has varied over time, a radiocarbon date, reported by a radiocarbon laboratory in radiocarbon years, is increasingly younger than calendar years beginning about 2,500 radiocarbon years ago. (Prior to this date, radiocarbon years generally are 50 to 100 years older.) For example, a radiocarbon date of 7000 B.P. actually is about 7800 B.P. in calendar years. Calibration scales have been developed for converting a radiocarbon date given in radiocarbon years to calendar years. However, these did not become readily available to archaeologists until the mid-1970s, so most North American regional chronologies based on radiocarbon dates are in terms of radiocarbon years rather than calendar years. Recently experts in radiocarbon dating have refined calibration scales; in particular, a separate calibration scale for dates derived from marine shell now exists, and a widely available computer program allows an archaeologist to input a raw, uncorrected radiocarbon date and its fractionation and reservoir corrections and receive a calibrated date and associated error factor (Stuiver and Braziunas 1993; Stuiver and Reimer 1993).

All of my references to dates in this study are in terms of radiocarbon years (except for dates in the historic period), and all are given as years B.P., or "before present," which by convention means before the calendar date of A.D. 1950. In other words, all of the dates in this study are *uncalibrated* as opposed to *calibrated*. I should mention, however, that it is becoming conventional in the archaeological literature to report both the uncorrected and uncalibrated "raw" radiocarbon date as well as the calibrated date. I have preferred to use radiocarbon years in this study for two reasons: first, nearly all of the existing regional chronologies in California are in terms of this time-scale; second, a chronology based on calibrated dates derived from shell implies greater precision than is justified in light of our poor understanding of the reservoir effect.

CROSS-DATING WITH ARTIFACTS

The other approach to assigning dates to Vandenberg site occupations, cross-dating with distinctive artifact forms, was applied mainly to the latter half of the 9,000-year prehistory of South Vandenberg. Of the several classes of time-sensitive artifacts found in Vandenberg sites, olivella shell beads were the most useful. I depended on a chronology of changing shell bead types that Chester King developed on the basis of bead associations with burials in dated Santa Barbara Channel cemeteries. An example of a chronologically distinctive bead type would be the money bead of the Chumash mentioned in Chapter 2, which apparently came into use about 800 B.P. but was not used prevalently until around 700 B.P. (Figure 2.3) Their presence, therefore, is indicative of occupation after 800 B.P., if not after 700 B.P. Another example is the so-called lipped bead, made from the outer wall of the olivella shell but including a small portion of the inner whorl or callus. Its presence indicates a date after about 450 B.P.–500 B.P. and spanning the first 100 years or so after initial European contact in A.D. 1542.

If a collection of shell beads from a site or a stratum within a site is large enough—say, in the order of 50 or more beads—it is often possible to date the occupation within a few hundred years, sometimes even more precisely if the occupation falls within the last 1,000 years of prehistory. However, the problem is that shell beads are usually quite rare in habitation deposits of sites earlier than about 1500 B.P., and there is practically no chance of obtaining a collection of this size from test excavations unless the site was occupied after around 600 B.P. With regard to the bead collections from sites excavated as part of the different phases of the Shuttle Project, it was possible only to date a site, or a stratigraphic division of a site, to a very broad division of time, several hundred to more than a thousand years long.

Another class of time-sensitive artifacts is projectile points. Before about 5000 B.P., however, distinctive forms of projectile points apparently did not exist, and those forms used later in time are not well dated. As well, complete or typeable fragments of projectile points typically are rare in sites, so they are frequently of little utility in establishing times of site occupation. Of the different forms of projectile points that occur in Vandenberg sites, the very small point forms are the most time-sensitive. These are arrowpoints, and their presence indicates a date after about 1500 B.P. when the bow and arrow began to be used in most parts of California (Figure 2.3).

Types of milling implements also have some value in determining periods of site occupation. If a site contains relatively abundant metates and manos but no mortars and pestles, the chances are high that it was occupied sometime before about 5500 B.P. Unfortunately, metates and manos were used prevalently after this date as well, so it is possible that some sites containing only metates and manos post-date 5500 B.P. Mortars and pestles appear not to have been used prior to 5500 B.P., so their presence at least is indicative of a post-5500 B.P. date. A distinctive form of mortar, with flattened rims and rim diameters of sometimes more than 50 cm, occurs very late in prehistory, perhaps only after 700 B.P. (Figure 2.3).

For a variety of reasons, none of the time-sensitive artifacts occurring in Vandenberg sites is of great utility in assigning dates to site occupations. First, many are so rare that they usually are not encountered during excavation. Second, the dates for initial and last use frequently are not well established, often because of dating problems caused by rodent disturbance. Finally, some artifact forms have a relatively long duration and therefore provide only minimal temporal resolution. Consequently, cross-dating with time-sensitive artifacts is useful mainly as a supplement to radiocarbon dating. At a few sites, radiocarbon dates are either absent or too few to provide a confident picture of the span of occupation, and this is where cross-dating with time-sensitive artifacts has its greatest utility.

A CHRONOLOGICAL FRAMEWORK FOR THE ANALYSIS

The study of cultural change using the archaeological record of a region such as South Vandenberg obviously requires that dates be assigned to the occupations of the sites investigated. However, it should be clear from the prior discussion that a good deal of uncertainty may exist in knowing when a site was occupied. At some sites rodent burrowing has mixed deposits of markedly different times; at other sites a radiocarbon date was obtained from a sample of many small pieces of shell that may have come from temporally different occupations. More commonly, too few radiocarbon dates were obtained from a site to be confident of the full duration of an occupation, or in the case of sites occupied more than once, the duration of each of perhaps several occupations.

A related problem is that all the sites investigated, taken together, certainly do not represent a continuous record of occupation through the 9,000-year prehistory of the region. For an interval of time in the order of, say, 200 years, deposits may not exist at any of the sites excavated, or if they do, their contents may not be adequate for characterizing cultural systems of this interval of time.

Taking into consideration these various problems in gaining temporal resolution, I decided that the best course of action would be to work with relatively broad temporal divisions in creating a chronological framework for the data analysis. I assumed that the greater amount of time encompassed by a division, the less chance that vagaries in dating site occupations or the representativeness of site contents would result in faulty interpretations. Of course, the broader the divisions in a chronological framework, the less chance there is of discerning cultural change, so I was motivated to keep the temporal divisions as narrow as possible.

I decided to adapt for my purposes a chronological framework developed by Chester King (1990:26–44). This framework is based on the changing popularity through time of shell-bead and ornament types as well as changes in specific attributes of shell beads and ornaments. King developed this chronology through a seriation study of beads and ornaments associated with burials in prehistoric cemeteries in the Santa Barbara Channel region. The chronology is particularly attractive to me in that it may be construed to be independent of cultural development. All the other chronological frameworks used in coastal southern California are inextricably associated with inferences about the nature of cultural systems prevailing during particular time intervals. King's chronology also is attractive because it is tied far more closely to radiocarbon dates than other chronologies, all of which were developed before many radiocarbon dates were available.

King used his chronological framework to look at changes in social and political organization, which he argued are reflected in the use of beads and ornaments in mortuary practices. He argued that stylistic changes in beads and ornaments reflect social and political changes; nonetheless, one may use these stylistic changes purely as time-markers, without reference to the social or political changes that may have caused them. Consequently, his chronological framework may be used just as easily for studies of such topics as subsistence or technological change.

King's chronological framework contains three main divisions: the Early, Middle, and Late Periods. Each of the periods is divided further into three to five numbered phases, and some of the phases, particularly those in the later half of the chronology, are divided into lettered subphases. It is normally possible to assign a site occupation to a particular period with a collection of only a dozen or so beads, but to be able to assign a site occupation to a phase or subphase normally requires 50 or more—quantities usually found only in mortuary contexts. As I mentioned earlier, I used dates assigned to bead types (and other distinctive artifact forms) as a supplement to radiocarbon dating, particularly in situations where only a few radiocarbon dates pertain to a site or a site stratum. My adaptation of King's chronological framework is as follows:

Paleocoastal Period	9000–8500 B.P.
Initial Early Period	8500–6500 B.P.
Terminal Early Period	5000–3200 B.P.
Middle Period	3200–800 B.P.
Late Period	800 B.P.–Missionization

The earliest period is not represented in King's chronological framework because none of his data came from sites earlier than about 7500 B.P. The period's name is adapted from Michael Morrato's proposal that a Paleo-Coastal Tradition (a tradition being a distinctive type of culture) may have existed along the southern California coast between 11,000 B.P. and 8000 B.P. (Morrato 1984:104). However, I use the period name to refer to a narrower bracket of time and without any presumption of cultural characteristics. The Initial Early Period correlates with the first phase of King's Early Period, whereas the Terminal Early Period correlates with the last two phases. The gap of more than 1,000 radiocarbon years between these two periods reflects the absence of archaeological collections of sufficient size and diversity dating to this interval of time. Although radiocarbon dates from Vandenberg sites do fall within this interval, data associated with these dates is minimal. The Middle and Late Periods are as King defined them, although the date dividing the Terminal Early and Middle Periods is earlier than he now believes to be the case.

I assigned sites or portions of sites to one of the periods listed on the basis of radiocarbon dates and in a few instances shell bead and arrowpoint types. Several of the sites clearly were occupied during more than one period, and, in the case of sites with substantial depth of deposits, the periods correlate with depth divisions. My confidence in the dates of site occupations varies considerably. For sites where only one or two dates are available, such as is the case with most of the sites tested in 1974, I strongly suspect that the available date or dates may not be telling the whole chronological story. Moreover, the several dates for certain sites do not present a clear chronological picture. When I discuss the chronology of individual site occupations later on, the adage that an archaeologist always could use more chronological information will be abundantly obvious.

5

Results of the Excavations

INTRODUCTION

Before addressing the elements of the research design outlined in Chapter 3, I need to describe the nature of the excavations at each site considered in the analysis and present information concerning each site's depositional structure and chronology. As well, I find it necessary to consider each site's settlement context. In building an argument about how a site fits into a settlement system, I shall give particular attention to subsistence activities because much of the research design is concerned with subsistence and diet. However, arguments about settlement context typically rely on knowledge of activities concerned with manufacture and maintenance of tools and facilities, so I also include some discussion of the evidence for these activities.

Once my crew and I had excavated the initial 5 percent sample from the impact areas at the three sites that were the focus of the 1978–80 phase of excavations, we were aware that many of the presumptions about the dating and depositional complexity of the sites based on the data collected in 1974 were either incorrect or in need of modification. This is not surprising, of course, since a few test units and one or two radiocarbon dates seldom provide a precise picture of a site's chronology and stratification. Fortunately, the new information from the initial samples made the project more interesting, and we discovered that the sites were in many respects more relevant to the research design than envisioned at the onset of the excavations.

Excavation procedures followed essentially the same format at each of the three sites (see Chapter 3), although there were variations to accommodate special circumstances. When the sample size was increased in most impact areas from the initial 5 percent to approximately 20 percent, the 1 m intervals along a baseline were placed in groups of five. Another interval would be selected at random from each group in which a unit had not already been excavated. Units in the initial 5 percent samples were excavated in 10 cm arbitrary levels (usually measured from a unit datum) until very few cultural items were encountered in a level. After we completed the 5 percent samples, most additional units were excavated in 20 cm levels because the degree of rodent disturbance encountered did not justify the greater effort required to excavate in finer vertical divisions. If soils were stratified, an arbitrary level in which a stratigraphic division was recognized was split in two along the stratigraphic division. The point at which excavation stopped in a unit usually was 1.0 m to 1.5 m below the surface, within a "sterile" soil horizon normally containing rodent burrows filled with soil from the midden deposits above (the filled burrows are krotovina—see discussion in Chapter 1).

In addition to the units excavated as part of the probability samples, some excavations took place in the impact areas to investigate features or to collect certain kinds of data. Because reasons for such excavations outside the probability samples varied, they will be considered under discussions of the investigations at each of the three sites.

Procedures for screening of deposits from the initial 5 percent samples entailed use of eighth-inch mesh and sorting of all materials caught by the screens in the field laboratory after washing. However, our budget would not allow continuing to sort all the eighth-inch screen residues derived from excavations beyond the 5 percent samples. Consequently, these deposits were initially screened through eighth-inch mesh and later rescreened through quarter-inch mesh. The materials caught by the quarter-inch mesh screens were washed and sorted in the field laboratory immediately after excavation, but the materials that had fallen through the quarter-inch mesh screens (and been caught by the eighth-inch mesh screens) were stored in case time became available later to sort these materials. Although very little time eventually could be devoted to this task, the 5 percent samples of the items between one-eighth and one-quarter of an inch in size were in most regards sufficient for the analysis.

SBA-539, SOUTH HONDA CANYON ROAD CUT

Excavation Details

The impact area at SBA-539 in which our excavations took place was about 5 m wide and 33 m long (Figure 5.1). Two episodes of excavation took place during the 1979–80 phase: the first during the winter of 1978–79 within the 2 m nearest to the existing road cut and the second during the summer of 1979, after surveyors for the U.S. Army Corps of Engineers corrected an error in their earlier survey that widened the impact area by another 3 m. Our excavations included an area of 26 m^2 and a total volume of 12.8 m^3. About 11 percent of the expanded impact area was excavated, and the excavated area is about 2 percent of the total site area.

The excavations along the impact area form a roughly north-south transect through the central portion of the site, where cultural remains appear to be the densest. Those units excavated before the impact area was expanded were the typical 1 m×2 m size, but those excavated in the expanded impact area were normally 1 m×1 m in size in order to disperse the sample as much as possible within the impact area, respecting time and money constraints operating at that time.

After completing formal excavations in the impact area before it was expanded, we shoveled much of the remaining midden deposits by 2 m intervals along the baseline into the back of a pickup truck (about a dozen loads altogether), transported the deposits to the field lab, sifted them through a large half-inch mesh screen with the aid of water, and rapidly sorted through the materials retained in the screen to recover large artifacts (such as chert preforms, projectile points, and sea mammal bones). In February 1980, a bucket and crane removed the remaining midden deposits in the expanded impact area under the watchful eye of an archaeologist looking for any distinctive features or human burials. A few larger artifacts also were collected during this operation, but of course the likelihood of recognizing artifacts under such circumstances is minimal.

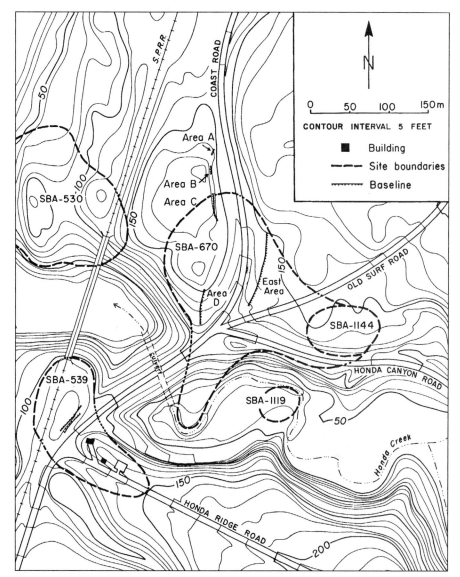

FIGURE 5.1   *Topographic context of sites SBA-539, 670, and nearby sites and locations of impact area baselines.*

Stratification of Deposits and Chronology

Stratification of deposits at SBA-539 is relatively uncomplicated (Figure 5.2). The upper 30 cm of midden deposits appear to have been significantly disturbed as a result of a variety of historic activities within the last 50 to 75 years, perhaps associated with a gravel road that passes just west of the impact area or the Southern Pacific Railroad, which cuts through the site 20 m beyond this road. A wide variety of fragmentary metal and glass objects in the upper 30 cm of midden deposits indicates that this up-

KEY

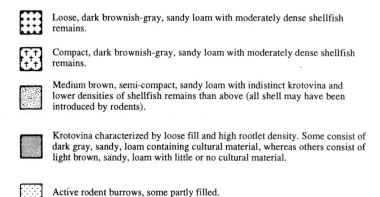

Loose, dark brownish-gray, sandy loam with moderately dense shellfish remains.

Compact, dark brownish-gray, sandy loam with moderately dense shellfish remains.

Medium brown, semi-compact, sandy loam with indistinct krotovina and lower densities of shellfish remains than above (all shell may have been introduced by rodents).

Krotovina characterized by loose fill and high rootlet density. Some consist of dark gray, sandy, loam containing cultural material, whereas others consist of light brown, sandy, loam with little or no cultural material.

Active rodent burrows, some partly filled.

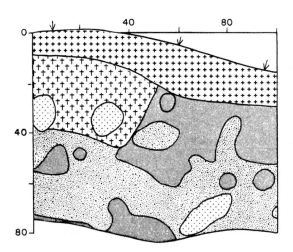

FIGURE 5.2 *Sidewall profile of an excavation unit at SBA-539 showing stratification of deposits.*

permost stratum probably has been churned, which probably accounts for the friability of its soil. Due to rodent disturbance, the division is not distinct between the uppermost stratum and the underlying stratum of relatively intact midden deposits. The intact midden stratum, which was more compact than the overlying stratum but was the same gray-brown color, extended to a maximum depth of 1.1 m below surface. It was in the intact midden stratum that cultural remains were densest. The combined thickness of the two midden strata was less near the existing road cut and toward the northern edge of the impact area. The lowermost stratum was medium-brown clayey soil containing many krotovina created by rodent burrowing.

The three radiocarbon dates obtained from shell samples are as follows:

¹⁴C yrs B.P.	Corrected Date B.P.	Depth (cm)	Material Dated
2500±70	2305	10–20	Calif. mussel shell fragments
2250±100	2055	40–50	Same as above
2110±70	1915	90–100	1 large piece of abalone shell

As can be seen, the three dates are in reverse order stratigraphically. However, if each date is considered an interval of time determined by the counting error (e.g., the lowermost date would be 2040 B.P.–2180 B.P.), there is comparatively little difference between them. The intervals represented by the two lowermost dates actually overlap, and only 80 years separate the intervals represented by the middle and upper dates. Treating the dates as intervals of time and correcting them for fractionation and reservoir effects, it is not unreasonable to conclude that occupation of SBA-539 probably took place sometime between 1845 B.P. and 2380 B.P. Yet this conclusion overlooks the fact that two of the dates were obtained from samples consisting of a few dozen pieces of California mussel shell. The difference between the oldest and youngest piece of shell in each sample is unknown, and the difference could be significant, even more than the interval of time represented by the counting error. At least it can be said, however, that SBA-539 was occupied over a period of a few hundred years, although not necessarily at the same level of intensity throughout this period.

Two of the 34 shell beads in the collections from SBA-539 are of a type known as the olivella cup (Figure 5.3). Made from the callus of the olivella shell, this type is known to date after about 800 B.P. Although none of the radiocarbon dates indicate such a late use of the site, the presence of these two beads leaves little question that the site witnessed ephemeral occupation after about 800 B.P. Aside from the beads, no other artifact types are associated definitively with this late period of occupation. In fact, cross-dates based on other artifact forms are consistent with the radiocarbon dates. These artifacts include olivella disk beads (made from the wall of the shell and having relatively large perforations) and relatively large contracting-stem points. No stratigraphic patterns in the depth distributions of the artifacts or other cultural remains could be discerned, implying that no significant cultural change took place during the occupation of SBA-539.

With regard to the chronological periods defined in Chapter 4, nearly all of the deposits at SBA-539 are a result of occupation during the Middle Period, but there appears to have been very limited use of the site during the Late Period as well.

Food Procurement and Consumption at SBA-539

Projectile points, shell fishhooks, and a cobble weight are artifacts associated with food procurement (Figure 5.3). Faunal remains are largely products of food consumption and include marine shells and bones of sea mammals, land mammals, fish, and birds.

Nearly all of the 26 points are fragmentary, but 12 are complete enough to identify them as dart points, although some could be harpoon points for hunting sea mammals.

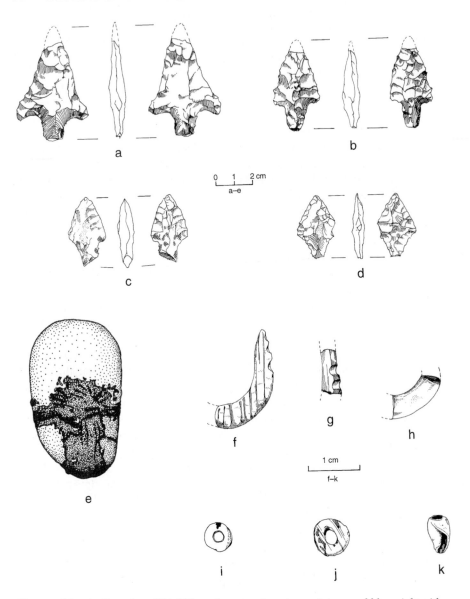

FIGURE 5.3 *Artifacts from SBA-539. a–d: contracting-stem points; e: cobble weight with adhering asphaltum for securing a line to the cobble; f–g: mussel shell fishhook fragments with notched shanks for attachment to a line; h: mussel shell fishhook fragment from near the incurved point; i–j: abalone and olivella shell disk beads; k: relatively small olivella spire-ground bead.*

In fact, 83 percent of the weight of mammal bone from excavated units identifiable at least to the family taxonomic level is of seals and sea lions (Phocidae and Otari-idae, respectively). Bones of California sea lion *(Zalophus californianus)* contribute

75 percent of the total weight, indicating an obvious focus on sea lion hunting. By contrast, mule deer *(Odocoileus hemionus)* contribute 10.5 percent, and various species of rabbits contribute 1.8 percent.

Three of the five mussel shell fishhook fragments retain at least portions of the notched shank to which line would have been attached. The hooks indicate that occupants of the site used hook-and-line to fish, probably from nearby rocky promontories that allow access to deep pools. The cobble weight mentioned above has asphaltum (tar) adhering to the unmodified cobble to aid in holding in place the cord wrapped around it. It may have been used to weight a fish line, although it could just as easily have served as a net weight.

Fish bone is relatively rare in the deposits. The comparatively few taxa represented by the identifiable fish bone are dominated by sardines and/or anchovies (order Clupeiformes), their vertebrae equaling 86.5 percent of the 650 identifiable bones. However, most or perhaps all of the vertebrae of these small fish could have come to the site as the stomach contents of hunted sea mammals. Alternatively, sardines and anchovies may have been acquired with nets, but this seems unlikely. Sardines and anchovies are not known to come so close to shore along the California coast that they could be acquired without boats. However, boats for gaining access to waters beyond the surf zone probably were not used by the site's inhabitants, if their lack along the Vandenberg coast at the time of European contact is any indication (see Chapter 2). Nonetheless, I must acknowledge that we know little about the behavior of these small fishes in nearshore waters prior to their intensive harvesting during historic times. They may have ranged into the surf zone prehistorically, much as they do today along the Peruvian coast (Quilter and Stocker 1983:548–549).

If we discount the sardine/anchovy vertebrae, surfperches *(Amphistichus* spp.) equal 56.8 percent of the total count, followed by cabezon *(Scorpaenichthys marmoratus),* 26.1 percent, and rockfishes *(Sebastes* spp.), 14.8 percent. These fishes inhabit the deep pools adjacent to rocky promontories.

Bird bone also is rare in the assemblage of faunal remains. Twenty-five of the 33 bird bones identifiable to family or genus are of three species of cormorants *(Phalacrocorax* spp.), very common marine birds along the Vandenberg coast. The remaining bird bones are of terrestrial or freshwater species. Not all of these birds necessarily were obtained for their food value. For instance, the Chumash made cloaks from the feathered skins of cormorants, and of course colorful feathers may have been used in various forms of decoration. No artifacts in the assemblage obviously were used to acquire birds. We may speculate that the site's inhabitants used traps, snares, or perhaps nets to capture both marine and freshwater birds.

As is typical of Vandenberg sites, California mussel *(Mytilus californianus)* accounts for more than 95 percent of the shellfish remains—in this case 97.5 percent. Excluding the barnacles, which probably came to the site attached to mussel shells, turbans *(Tegula* spp.) and abalones *(Haliotis* spp.) are next in importance behind mussel. All of these shellfish are found attached to rocks in the lower intertidal zone, and prime shellfish-collecting locales are within a kilometer southwest of the site at Point Pedernales. Very rare at SBA-539 are shells of littleneck clams *(Protothaca staminea)* and pismo clams *(Tivela stultorum).* Littleneck clams inhabit coarse gravels under loose rocks in the lower intertidal zone, and pismo clams are buried several inches in the lower intertidal zone of sandy beaches. Gravelly shoals and sandy beaches are very near SBA-539.

The only cultural remains from SBA-539 indicative of plant food consumption are artifacts used to mill seeds or nuts. A metate fragment, a mano, and two small fragments of manos indicate that small seeds were collected and milled into flour, while a complete pestle and four pestle fragments reflect acorn processing. A variety of seeds from grasses and annuals probably were collected from grasslands or streamsides very near SBA-539, but acorns probably were imported from locations several kilometers inland, perhaps in the upper reaches of Honda Canyon.

The Settlement Context of SBA-539

Between about 1,900 and 2,300 years ago SBA-539 appears to have been the principal locus of occupation by people taking advantage of resources at or near the mouth of Honda Canyon, including fresh water and various riparian resources. Neighboring sites in the cluster of four located at or near the mouth of Honda Canyon, specifically SBA-530 and 670, are not known to have extensive deposits dating to this period of time, although SBA-530 does contain some deposits dating within this bracket of time. Interestingly, SBA-539 is the only site in the cluster overlooking the canyon from its south edge, a location perhaps reflecting the interests of its occupants in resource areas south of the site.

Based on a variety of artifacts associated with manufacture and maintenance activities, some of which are abundant in the artifact assemblage, SBA-539 probably was a residential base occupied by groups composed of both males and females, that is, by complete family units. The area of relatively dense midden deposits at SBA-539 is no more than 100 m in length. If we assume that this is the area where habitation actually took place, it seems reasonable to argue that a population of 10 to 20 individuals occupied the site.

Knapping stone tools was one of the most prominent classes of activities that took place at SBA-539. Waste flakes of local chert, called Monterey chert after the name of the bedrock formation in which it is found, are the product of knapping activities. They are in densities of more than 3,100 flakes per cubic meter at SBA-539. Tabular cobbles of chert may be found today in the streambed at the bottom of Honda Canyon, as well as on cobble beaches southwest of the site.

Flaked stone artifacts include 74 cores, from which flakes were struck for use in such tasks as butchering mammals. A total of 101 flake tools were identified on the basis of unifacial edge damage or retouch, but probably many more were discarded before their edges began to show visible use-wear. There are also 74 chert biface preforms in the flaked stone collection. The analysis of waste flakes from SBA-539 revealed that most or all of the preforms were initially shaped at a location other than SBA-539, probably near the source of the chert. Curiously, the waste flakes include very few biface thinning flakes resulting from the final stages of knapping preforms into finished projectile points or knives. It would seem, therefore, that only the intermediate stages of point manufacture took place at SBA-539. Much of the manufacture of flaked stone tools was done with cobble hammerstones, there being 27 in the artifact collections.

The pattern in the nature of preforms and waste flakes at SBA-539 implies geographic segregation of different segments of the biface manufacturing process as well as finished tool use. Knappers occupying SBA-539 may have prepared biface preforms and transported them to another site, such as a winter residential base, where they completed manufacturing of projectile points or knives. They eventually returned to SBA-539, where they used the finished tools in such activities as hunting and butchering. As well, they once again knapped preforms to an intermediate stage of their reduction.

Tarring the interior surface of baskets to make them waterproof was another significant activity undertaken at SBA-539. Ethnographic information on the Chumash and other native California groups includes descriptions of how basketry containers were tarred. Nodules of hard asphaltum obtained from tar seeps were placed in a basketry bottle along with pebbles heated in a fire. The asphaltum nodules and pebbles were shaken, which caused the hot pebbles to acquire a coating of melted asphaltum. This coating then rubbed off on the interior sides of the basketry bottle. Once the pebbles were poured out and the asphaltum allowed to cool, the basket's interior was covered with a durable, waterproof coating. Pebbles retaining a coating of tar are the archaeological manifestation of this practice, and 27 tarring pebbles, as they are called, are in the artifact collections from SBA-539. Of course, small chunks of asphaltum recovered from the site surely are related to this activity, but tar also is known to have been used as a fixative or glue. For instance, the cord tied around the cobble weight mentioned earlier was held in place with asphaltum. Recovered from SBA-539 were 115.5 grams of asphaltum, much of it in very small chunks.

While knapping of preforms could be argued to have been practiced by males at practically any convenient location, including both residential bases and temporary camps of various sorts, preparing asphaltum and tarring baskets would be convenient only at a residential base. The dark color of the midden soil at SBA-539 and the ubiquity of charcoal flecks, produced by frequent use of hearth fires, also are indicative of the longer-term occupation expectable at a residential base. Another strong piece of circumstantial evidence indicative of longer-term residential use of SBA-539 is the presence of a burial of a ten-year-old child. Burials, particularly of children, are more likely to occur at a residential base than at a temporary camp.

Something may be said about the season or seasons when occupation took place. The great majority of sea lion bones are from males, the sex being easily determined by the large size of the skeletal elements. (The weight of live adult males is roughly three times that of adult females.) Information on the natural history of California sea lions reveals that males are scarce along the Vandenberg coast during early summer, when they are occupying rookeries on the Channel Islands to the south. Males reach their maximum density along the central California coast between late summer and the end of winter. Consequently, SBA-539 probably was occupied sometime during this interval of time. The presence of a bone identified to be from a surf scoter, a migratory bird that winters along the central California coast, also is indicative of winter occupation. It must be emphasized, however, that we can hypothesize when people probably were present at SBA-539 on the basis of this natural history information, not when they were absent.

SBA-670, NORTH HONDA CANYON ROAD CUT
Excavation Details

Excavation at SBA-670 initially took place along a series of three impact areas along the western side of the road cut passing through the site (Figure 5.1). The collection of the initial 5 percent sample revealed that the two northernmost impact areas were essentially sterile of cultural remains even though low-density scatters of chert flakes and shell fragments were in their vicinities. Consequently, all subsequent excavations were in the southernmost impact area, where the sample was increased to 16.7 percent. The total volume of excavated deposits in this impact area was 33.35 m³, and the total area excavated was 44.5 m², less than 1 percent of the site's large area. Furthermore, only the two test units excavated in 1974 were in the portion of the site with the highest concentrations of cultural remains. At the location of the southernmost impact area the densities of cultural remains were significantly lower.

The archaeological deposits of the southernmost impact area capped a dune hill through which Coast Road was cut. Each day we climbed the 15-m-high road cut to our excavations, and in the course of one of these struggles up the loose sand of the road cut I noticed that the sand was significantly darker and contained denser shellfish remains near the base of the road cut than farther up the slope. This seemed incongruous, because the darkness of the soil and the density of shellfish remains should be highest near the top of the road cut, where the site was located. I had a few of the field crew members scrape off the slough in the area where the dark soil and shellfish remains occurred near the base of the slope, and to our surprise we discovered a stratum of dark gray-brown shell midden about a meter thick (Figure 5.4). We traced the midden for a distance of about 50 m along the face of the road cut, and we found that it gradually merged with a buried soil stratum, the top of which we eventually identified as an ancient dune surface that had been buried by nearly 15 m of new dune sand. Of course, the midden we had discovered was buried at the same time.

As we shall see in the next chapter, this buried midden had implications for paleoenvironmental reconstruction. However, at the time of the discovery we were confronted with the problem of unanticipated deposits that would be disturbed by road cut widening. After we cleared the overlying dune sand, three pairs of units

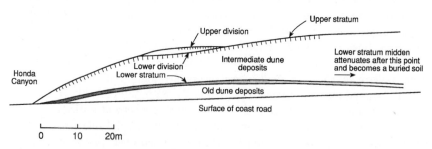

FIGURE 5.4 *Profile of dune and midden deposits seen along the road cut through SBA-670.*

PHOTO 5.1   *A profile of the lower midden stratum at SBA-670. The white flecks are shellfish remains. Note that there is a very distinct boundary between the shell midden and the dark sterile soil overlying it. The boundary between this dark sterile soil and the overlying dune sand also is quite distinct.*

were excavated, the pairs being spaced about 10 m apart. Because the eastern unit of each pair was truncated by the road cut, only the inner three units were essentially complete. Excavations in this lower midden stratum covered an area of 11 m² and equaled a volume of 7.68 m³.

After we completed the excavations at SBA-670 over the winter of 1978–79, the U.S. Army Corps of Engineers revised the centerline of the shuttlecraft tow route eastward to place all impacts on the east side of the road rather than the west. During the summer of 1979, therefore, a crew returned to SBA-670 and excavated five 1 m ×1 m units spaced at approximately equal intervals along the length of the impact area. Only about 0.8 percent of the impact area was excavated, but the very low densities of cultural remains did not justify a larger sample. Below a depth of 60 cm, the southernmost unit encountered the dark gray deposits of the lower midden stratum. The crew then traced the extent of this stratum along the eastern face of the road cut. In early February 1980, a bulldozer removed the overlying dune sands to within less than a half meter of the lower midden stratum, and a small crew excavated four 1 m×1 m units through the midden stratum. Although the stratum was the same dark dray color as that on the western side of the road cut, it contained much lower densities of flakes and only sporadic shellfish remains. Excavations in the lower midden stratum on the eastern side of the road equaled a volume of 7.7 m³. Of course, it is impossible to say what percentage of the total lower midden stratum was excavated since its areal extent is unknown.

Stratification of the Deposits and Chronology

Along the western face of the road cut, the midden stratum capping the dune hill, which I shall call the upper midden stratum, is separated from the lower midden stratum near the base of the road cut by 10 m to 15 m of sterile dune sands. In essence they are separate sites, although the site designation of SBA-670 embraces both.

In the southern half of the impact area, the stratification of upper midden stratum has some complexity. Near the northern extreme of the impact area the midden deposits are about 50 cm thick, and the thickness diminishes southwards. Near the center of the impact area, where the midden is only about 20 cm thick, the midden divides into an upper and lower segment. Southward from this point the upper segment continues to cap the dune as a low-density surface deposit, but the lower segment, remaining about 20 cm thick, plunges toward the south into the dune and is largely buried under as much as 2 m of sterile dune sand (Figure 5.5). However, radiocarbon dates indicate there is essentially no difference in time between the two segments, indicating that a short episode of dune movement must have taken place during the interval of time that people occupied the site. The radiocarbon dates pertaining to the upper midden stratum (including the upper and lower segments) are as follows:

^{14}C yrs B.P.	Corrected Date B.P.	Location	Depth (cm)	Material Dated
490±150	490	1974 unit in area of highest midden density	40–60	Wood charcoal
530±90	335	Near north end of impact area	20–65	California mussel shell fragments
590±100	395	Lower segment near south end	0–20	California mussel shell fragments

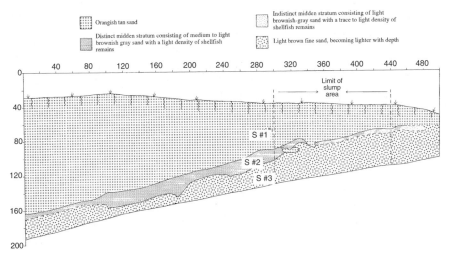

FIGURE 5.5 *Sidewall profile of an excavation unit into upper midden stratum deposits at SBA-670.*

There is no significant difference between these dates in either their uncorrected or corrected form. It appears that the upper midden stratum, including both segments in the southern sector of the impact area, represents a very short period of occupation very late in prehistory.

The five dates pertaining to the lower midden stratum are as follows:

^{14}C yrs B.P.	Corrected Date B.P.	Location	Depth (cm)	Material Dated
4340±80	4145	Southernmost unit pair	20–30	California mussel shell fragments
4780±80	4585	Southernmost unit pair	80–100	Same as above
3370±90	3175	Northernmost unit pair	10–20	Same as above
3935±110	3740	Northernmost unit pair	30–40	Same as above
3780±70	3585	Northernmost unit pair	70–80	Same as above

The dates from the southern end of the lower midden stratum are a good deal earlier than those from the northern end, there being 560 years separating the two sets. The two dates from the southernmost unit pair are separated by 440 years, while the oldest and youngest date from the northernmost unit pair are separated by 565 years. These are both considerable spans of time. However, the two dates from the intermediate and lower levels of the northernmost unit pair are so close to each other that their counting errors overlap. Consequently, the stratigraphic reversal of these two dates probably is insignificant.

Despite the lack of clear stratification of deposits, the lower midden stratum may be the result of two separate occupations. On the basis of so few dates spread over about 1,000 years, however, this conclusion should be treated as only one possibility.

The problem confronted in interpreting these five dates demonstrates the shortcoming of combining a dozen or more pieces of shell for one radiocarbon sample. Had only one shell comprised a sample, a clearer picture of the chronology of occupation undoubtedly would have emerged.

There are differences in the characteristics of the deposits between the northernmost and southernmost unit pairs. Shellfish remains and chert flakes were in much lower densities in the southernmost unit pair. Furthermore, midden in this unit pair and the middle unit pair was capped with about 10 cm of dark gray sand lacking cultural remains. This implies that sand mixed with soot and other fine organic matter was wind-transported southward from the vicinity of the northernmost unit pair, where occupation began around 3700 B.P., to the vicinity of the middle and southernmost unit pair, where occupation terminated about 4100 B.P. It is possible, therefore, that the area of occupation migrated northward through time and that the intensity of occupation increased as well. Proper evaluation of this interpretation, however, would require more chronological information than is currently available.

With a few minor exceptions, the artifacts serving as time-markers are consistent with the radiocarbon dates. The upper midden stratum yielded two olivella cup (callus) beads, a type dating to the beginning of the Late Period about 800 B.P. An olivella lipped bead blank, also from the upper midden stratum, indicates a date after 500 B.P. Two serpentine disk beads from the southernmost unit pair in the lower midden stratum are of a type spanning a period between 3400 B.P. and 1700 B.P. The earliest date of occurrence is about 700 years later than the latest radiocarbon date for this unit pair, an inconsistency that may have been caused by vagaries in the composition of the radiocarbon samples mentioned above. An olivella spire-ground bead from the lower midden stratum typically is the most common bead type present in habitation deposits dating throughout the Early Period.

Regarding time-sensitive projectile point types, a large side-notched point came from a unit on the east side of the road cut in the lower midden stratum. This type has been dated to about 5000 B.P. in the Santa Barbara Channel region (Figure 2.3). On the west side of the road cut, the northernmost unit pair in the lower midden stratum yielded three contracting-stem projectile points (Figure 5.6). The associated radiocarbon dates are consistent with the earliest known occurrence of this type. A contracting stem projectile point also came from the upper midden stratum, a context later than expected. Use of this type apparently terminated around 1500 B.P., and its presence in the upper midden stratum could mean that sporadic occupation occurred somewhat before this date, perhaps when SBA-539, on the opposite side of the canyon, was occupied. The terminal date of this point type is not well established, however, and it is possible that it was in sporadic use as late as 500 B.P.

With regard to the chronological periods defined in Chapter 4, dates for the upper midden stratum fall within the Late Period, and those for the lower midden stratum fall within the Terminal Early Period.

Food Procurement and Consumption at SBA-670

The upper midden stratum at SBA-670 yielded only one typeable point fragment and three untypeable fragments. These small numbers are at least partly the result of the

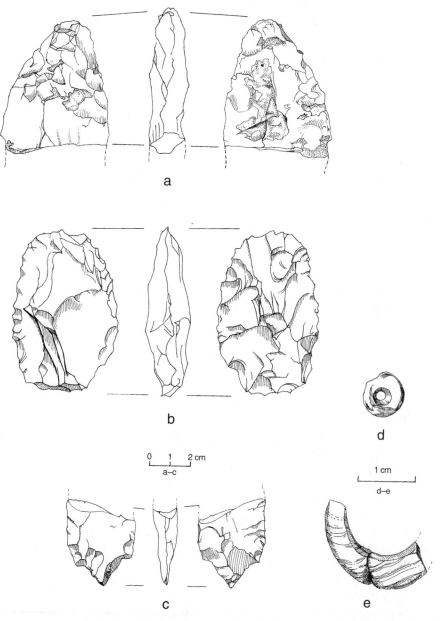

a

b

d

0   1   2 cm
a–c

1 cm
d–e

c

e

FIGURE 5.6 *Artifacts from SBA-670. a–b: preforms from the lower stratum; c: contracting-stem point from the lower stratum (short-stemmed points appear to be typical of a period around 4500 B.P.–4000 B.P. along the Santa Barbara Channel); d: olivella callus bead from the upper stratum; e: mussel shell fishhook fragment from the upper stratum.*

marginal position of the upper midden stratum impact areas. In contrast, the number of points from the lower midden stratum is rather high, considering the small volume of deposits excavated. Five typeable point fragments, all the size of dart points, and eight untypeable fragments are in the collections. However, as we will discuss later, manufacture of points was a major industry, so some of these points could be the result of discard because of errors during the final stage of point manufacture.

By weight, 90.9 percent of the bone from the upper midden stratum units identifiable to family or more specific taxon (104 out of 109 by count) is from small species of rabbits *(Sylvilagus* spp.), and none is from sea mammals. From the lower midden stratum only 3 of the 98 identifiable bones are from sea mammals, but because of their relatively large size they equal 68.1 percent of the total weight. By contrast, 70 of the 98 bones are from small rabbits, but they equal only 13.5 percent of the total weight. This confusing picture of weight versus count of identifiable bone exposes some of the problems that arise if one depends on only one or the other when the sample size is numerically small. Regardless, rabbits clearly were more important to the inhabitants of SBA-670, and sea mammals less important, than these taxa were to the inhabitants of SBA-539.

Occupants of SBA-670 during the Terminal Early Period obtained birds from both freshwater and marine habitats. As was the case at SBA-539, cormorants dominate the assemblage of bird bones identifiable at least to family; they account for 13 of the 21 identifiable bones. The remaining 8 identified bones are divided between marine and freshwater birds.

Only 9 bird bones were recovered from the upper midden stratum in the impact area, largely because it was marginal to the denser midden concentrations. However, the test units excavated in 1974 yielded an unusual variety of avian species, there being 26 taxa represented. Cormorants account for 54 of the 89 identified bones, following the general pattern discussed above. Other relatively prominent marine taxa are four species of gulls *(Larus* spp.), equaling 7 bones, and two species of scoters *(Melanitta* spp.), equaling 6 bones. Terrestrial birds represented by 1 or 2 bones per taxa include red-tailed hawk *(Buteo jamaicensis),* great horned owl *(Bubo virginianus),* and California quail *(Lophortyx californicus).* Freshwater birds, also represented by 1 or 2 bones per taxon, include common loon *(Gavia immer),* American coot *(Fulica americana),* eared grebe *(Podiceps caspicus),* and brant *(Branta bernicla).*

Considering that all of these avian remains came from two test units equaling a total volume of only 4.5 m^3, this is an impressive quantity of avian bone. The diversity, however, may be simply the result of a numerically much larger sample of bird bones. Nonetheless, one may conclude that capture of birds along the coastal shoreline, in marsh or freshwater habitats and in terrestrial habitats, certainly was a serious enterprise during the Late Period occupation of SBA-670. Probably a variety of capture methods were used, including nets, snares and traps, and bare hands.

Four shell fishhook fragments from the upper midden stratum reveal that Late Period occupants of SBA-670 fished with hook and line (Figure 5.6). Considering that three of these fragments came from the impact area, which is marginal to the area of dense midden deposits, fishhooks may be relatively abundant in the upper midden stratum. Similar to the pattern seen at SBA-539, 68 of the 92 taxonomically identified fish bones are of sardines and anchovies, and the remaining bones are of taxa such as surfperches and rockfishes that could be caught with hook-and-line from rocky promontories. The sardine and anchovy bones may be from the stomach contents of seals and sea lions even though none are present among the identified mammal bones from the upper midden stratum. I will discuss in Chapter 7, however, a column sample from one of the 1974 test units that did include quantities of sea mammal bone that could not be identified to a particular taxon.

No fishhooks and only four fish bones came from the lower midden stratum. The small quantities of fish bone are partly the result of the fact that the assemblage includes bones no smaller than what would be caught by quarter-inch mesh screens. It does appear, however, that fishing was not as important a subsistence pursuit during the Terminal Early Period occupation of SBA-670 as it was during the Late Period occupation.

The shellfish assemblages from the two midden strata are broadly similar, but there are some interesting differences. California mussel is 98.3 percent of the total weight in the lower midden stratum, while it is 94.8 percent of the total in the upper midden stratum. As we shall see in Chapter 7, the lower percentage of mussel and the relatively higher percentage of small shellfish species, particularly the turbans, is typical of Late Period sites. Regardless of the differences, occupants of SBA-670 during both time periods focused their shellfish collecting on the rocky intertidal zone, although they did occasionally acquire clams from sand or gravel beaches.

Use of plant foods is reflected by two mano fragments, two metate or mortar fragments, and a globular mortar fragment, all from the lower midden stratum. The absence of such artifacts in the assemblage from the upper midden stratum probably is due to the very low frequencies of artifacts of any type in the marginal deposits where the impact areas were located.

The Settlement Contexts of SBA-670

The comparatively small sizes of the collections from the two midden strata of SBA-670 make it difficult to infer the kind of settlement the site was during the two periods of occupation. However, the variety of artifacts and waste products associated with manufacturing and maintenance activities from both midden strata does imply that the site served as a residential base during both occupations.

As was the case at SBA-539, both midden strata at SBA-670 yielded evidence of working with asphaltum and tarring the insides of basketry water bottles. This testifies to the long prehistory of this technology in the Vandenberg region. The upper midden stratum yielded five tarring pebbles and 183.1 g of asphaltum chunks. The small number of tarring pebbles is expectable in light of the marginal nature of the deposits where excavation took place, but the quantity of asphaltum is unusually large, implying that asphaltum chunks are quite dense in the main part of the upper midden stratum. The lower midden stratum yielded four tarring pebbles and 85.0 g of asphaltum chunks, a relatively substantial amount considering the small volume of excavated deposits.

A very significant industrial focus during the Terminal Early Period occupation of SBA-670 was the production of biface preforms, there being 51 in the lower midden stratum collections (Figure 5.6). At more than 6 preforms per cubic meter, the density of broken or rejected preforms in the lower midden stratum is unusually high. Biface preforms also were produced during Late Period times at SBA-670, but not at the same level of intensity. As would be expected, waste flake densities in the lower midden stratum also are very high, with a maximum density of 5,516.4 flakes per cubic meter (5,023.5 g/m³). The maximum density in the upper stratum impact areas is only 141.1 flakes per cubic meter (62.6 g/m³), but from one of the 1974 test units in the main part of the site the density is 708.3 flakes per cubic meter (908 g/m³), still substantially below the density in the lower midden stratum. Arnold's analysis of the preforms and waste flakes from the Shuttle Project sites revealed that Terminal Early Period preform reduction at SBA-670 was largely restricted to the middle stages of point manufacture, as was the case at SBA-539.

Production of flake tools from chert cores appears not to have been a significant activity during either Late or Terminal Early Period occupations. Only three chert cores came from the upper midden stratum, and only five came from the lower midden stratum. Nonetheless, the 124 utilized and retouched flakes from the Terminal Early Period deposits is a relatively high quantity, perhaps because flakes from preform reduction rather than from cores were used. It is also possible that many utilized flakes really are not utilized. Utilized flakes were classified as such if a continuous series of minute unifacial flake scars was observed along an edge. Although this type of edge damage probably is the result of use of the flake to scrape against a hard material such as wood or bone, it may be created accidentally. The incidence of accidental edge damage should correlate with the abundance of flakes, which of course is large in the lower midden stratum. The upper midden stratum yielded only 27 utilized or retouched flakes.

Considering how important preform knapping was during the Terminal Early Period occupation of SBA-670, it is curious that hammerstones are absent from the artifact assemblage. Moreover, the only hammerstone from the upper midden stratum is a core type, which probably was not used for knapping. Hammers may have been hardwood billets, which of course would not survive to be part of the archaeological record. Alternatively, it is possible that very few hammerstones were used to produce the high density of flakes in the lower midden stratum, so the chances of encountering a hammerstone are small. This possibility has some credence because cobble hammerstones, the type that would be used for knapping, are typically rare in Vandenberg sites. Nonetheless, in light of the high density of flakes, I would expect at least a few hammerstones if they were used for knapping, so I favor the first possibility.

The composition and size of the social groups occupying SBA-670 during the two periods of occupation is difficult to infer from the available data. The variety of subsistence remains and the diversity of artifacts associated with manufacture and maintenance activities implies that family groups occupied the site during both periods. However, reduction of chert preforms undoubtedly was an exclusively male enterprise, and the abundant evidence of this industry could mean occupation by males only. Such a conclusion is unwarranted, however, since reduction of just one serviceable preform produces a few hundred waste flakes and perhaps a few rejected preforms as well. Consequently, while the lower midden stratum artifact assemblage looks like it is heavily weighted toward male activities, it really is not.

A few lines of circumstantial evidence provide some clues regarding length of site occupation during an annual cycle of movement. In both midden strata at SBA-

670, bone, shell, and charcoal are highly fragmented and evenly dispersed compared to the situation at many other Vandenberg sites. This implies that the middens are the result of many short-term occupations with enough time between occupations for weathering of these materials to take place. The lack of distinct features such as hearths or lenses of ashy midden also implies that months of time passed before the site again was occupied. This line of reasoning is based on my general knowledge of midden deposits in the Vandenberg region and neighboring regions, and I have not had the opportunity to develop quantitative measures of such differences in midden constituents.

Because Late Period occupants of SBA-670 placed some emphasis on fishing, it seems likely that residence at the site occurred during the summer months, when surf would have been relatively quiet and the weather more amenable. However, a few of the species represented in the bird bone, including the loons, eared grebe, and the scoters, normally are present only during winter months. Their bones, therefore, imply winter occupation. During the Late Period, SBA-670 may have been occupied intermittently throughout the year as particular food resources became available or accessible. During the Terminal Early Period, the site appears to have been occupied at times during winter months, but available data do not allow more to be said about seasonality of occupation.

SBA-931, SURF ROAD CUT

Excavation Details

SBA-931 is located just east of the former Southern Pacific Railroad depot of Surf, and the site deposits cover a series of knolls overlooking the mouth of the Santa Ynez River from the south. The site differs from SBA-539 and 670 in a number of respects. Shellfish remains and many other cultural remains are in much lower densities, and the archaeological deposits are not the classic shell midden found at many other Vandenberg sites. Indeed, one must have a sharp eye to recognize SBA-931 as a site while walking over its surface. Yet SBA-931 contains densities of ground stone artifacts much higher than at SBA-539 and 670, and certain tool types are present at SBA-931 that are absent at SBA-539 and 670.

We devoted most of our excavation effort to SBA-931, where the impact areas were larger and stratification of deposits was the most difficult to unravel. Units were excavated in four impact areas, labeled Areas A through D (Figure 5.7). Areas A, B, and C were along the south side of the road serving as the shuttlecraft tow route, and Area D was along the north side, directly opposite Area C. Short ravines divide the Areas A, B, and C, so each runs along the crest of a knoll with ravines on one or both sides.

As a result of excavating the initial 5 percent sample, Area D was eliminated from further consideration, because it contained very low densities of cultural remains on a relatively steep slope that had risen to the top edge of the bluff prior to road construction in the 1960s. Area C also contained relatively low densities of cultural remains, and most excavation after the initial 5 percent sample was devoted to

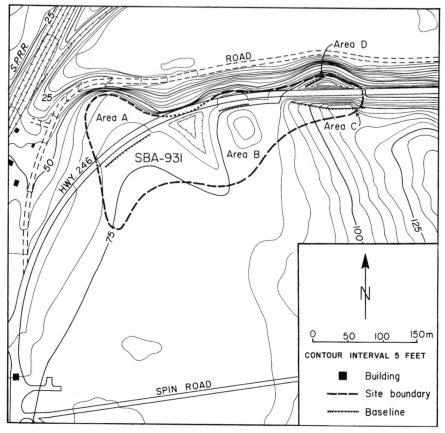

FIGURE 5.7 *Topographic context of SBA-931 and locations of impact area baselines.*

exposing a spectacular roasting-pit feature. This pit had fire-reddened sides and was filled to its brim with fire-altered rocks (Figure 5.8 and Photo 5.2). The highest density of cultural remains was discovered toward the eastern end of Area A, and a moderate density also was encountered in Area B.

In an effort to discern patterns in the areal distributions of cultural items, as well as to understand better the relationship between two soil strata, I decided to open a 4 m×12 m area near the eastern end of Area A. The initial 5-percent sample revealed that this portion of the site contained the highest densities of artifacts, which I reasoned would provide the best opportunities for stratigraphy and identification of patterning in areal distributions.

Above a depth of 60 cm in the 4 m×12 m area, units were 2 m×2 m in size and levels were 20 cm thick. Below, units were 1 m×1 m in size and levels were 10 cm thick, and the excavation crew recorded the three-dimensional position of each cultural item longer than 3 cm. At a depth of 80 cm to 90 cm was the top of a very distinct stratum consisting of a compact, light-colored soil containing relatively abundant small fragments of mussel shell (Figure 5.9). This lower stratum was extensively disturbed

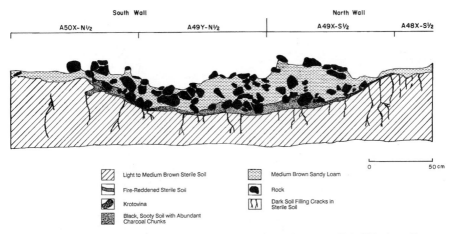

South Wall   North Wall

A5OX-N½   A49Y-N½   A49X-S½   A48X-S½

0   50 cm

- Light to Medium Brown Sterile Soil
- Fire-Reddened Sterile Soil
- Krotovina
- Black, Sooty Soil with Abundant Charcoal Chunks
- Medium Brown Sandy Loam
- Rock
- Dark Soil Filling Cracks in Sterile Soil

FIGURE 5.8   *Profile through the center of the roasting-pit feature at SBA-931, Area C.*

by rodent burrowing, and krotovina consisted of relatively friable soil, medium brown in color. In an effort to separate the two soil strata, the krotovina in the lower stratum were excavated while leaving the compact lower stratum in place. This effort was only partly successful, because many krotovina were a mixture of soils from the two strata and could not always be easily discerned.

The roasting-pit feature in Area C was excavated as an areal exposure in much the same manner, although the area of excavation was not much larger than the area of the feature. However, here the stratigraphic distinction was between an overburden 20 cm–30 cm thick and the rock-and-ash-filled contents of the roasting pit. A continuous series of 1 m×2 m units was excavated in Area B, but this was not treated as an areal exposure. Its purpose was simply to increase the size of the sample of cultural items from this area.

The total amount of excavation in the different areas of SBA-931 are summarized as follows:

Area	Excavated Area, m^2	% of Total Area	Excavated Volume, m^3
A	147.5	27.3	93.50
B	64.3	23.1	42.24
C	75.3	22.5	37.21
D	9.0	3.8	6.34

Stratification of Deposits and Chronology

The deposits of Area A contained the clearest stratigraphic distinctions and therefore provided the basis for distinguishing between the two principal occupations of SBA-931. Expanding the brief description above, the upper stratum consists of a medium

PHOTO 5.2   *The exposure of the upper surface of a roasting pit feature at SBA-931, Area C. The strings delineate 1 m×1 m units. Most of the rocks filling the roasting pit are fire-altered as a result of their use as a source of heat for roasting.*

brown, sandy loam that was easy to excavate, whereas the underlying stratum consists of a tan-colored sand containing a moderately high density of very small fragments of marine shells—mostly of mussel. This lower stratum was quite compact and difficult to excavate when dry due to partial cementation by calcium carbonate derived from the shellfish remains. Rodent burrowing has been extensive in both strata, and rodents have moved shells from the lower stratum upward into the upper stratum, which appears not to have contained much shell originally. As Don Johnson's analysis of SBA-931 soils demonstrates, the ground water percolating downward through the soil profile has leached the calcium carbonate from the shell, which was then deposited in the lower stratum and the sterile soil below it.

The lower stratum in Area A has been dated to a period around 8300 B.P.–9000 B.P., making it the earliest archaeological deposit so far known in the Vandenberg region. Sometime after this initial occupation of SBA-931, aeolian sands began to accumulate, and the site was eventually reoccupied. It is possible that this second reoccupation continued intermittently at the same time that more sand was blown onto the site. Moreover, sand may have continued to accumulate after the second occupation terminated. At any rate, the highest densities of cultural remains associated with this second occupation are between 60 cm and 80 cm in depth. However, some of the con-

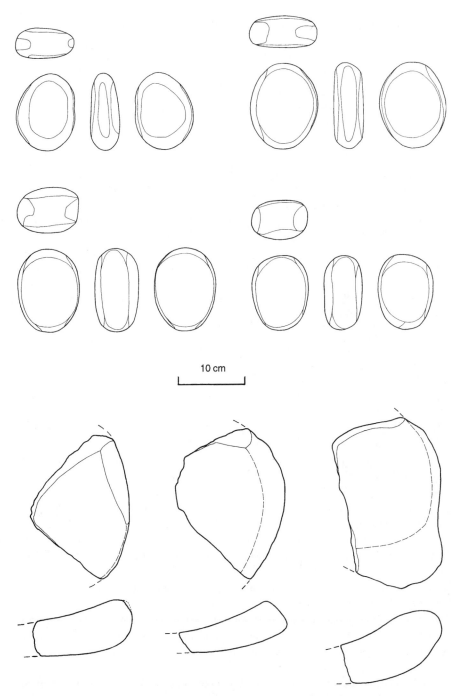

10 cm

FIGURE 5.10 *Manos and metates from SBA-931 and 552. above: bifacial, edge-ground manos (fine lines show the perimeters of abraded surfaces); below: metate rim fragments (dashed lines show the perimeters of abraded surfaces).*

it provides little chronological information. The near absence of beads, however, is more typical of occupation during the Early Period, prior to 3000 B.P.

A fragment of a plumb-shaped artifact referred to as a "charmstone" by California archaeologists (or sometimes plummet-stone) is similar in form and of the same material as one from a Santa Barbara Channel site dating around 5000 B.P. This also came from the upper stratum of Area A.

A relatively large expanding-stem (or corner-notched) projectile point from the upper stratum of Area A appears to be a type dating about 5000 B.P. in the Santa Barbara Channel region (Figure 5.11). Two contracting-stem points, one from the upper stratum of Area A and another from Area C (some distance from the roasting-pit feature), apparently were used between 4500 B.P. and 1500 B.P. A small, concave base point from Area C, probably an arrow point, undoubtedly dates after 700 B.P.

This somewhat confusing array of time-marker artifacts appears to indicate that the upper midden stratum of Areas A and B probably dates to a period around 5000 B.P. and that ephemeral occupation of SBA-931 took place throughout the rest of prehistory. This is not surprising in light of the geographic location of the site. Overlooking the mouth of the Santa Ynez River, it provided access to marshland resources and probably fresh water, and people passing between the coast and the upper reaches of the Santa Ynez Valley probably crossed the site frequently.

Food Procurement and Consumption at SBA-931

Projectile points are the only class of artifacts from SBA-931 directly related to food procurement. The upper stratum of Areas A and B yielded 6 typeable points that may have tipped darts and 27 untypeable point fragments. The lower stratum of Area A yielded only 1 fragment that proved to be untypeable. Area C yielded a small point that probably tipped an arrow and 1 untypeable fragment. The number of points is small considering the large volume of excavated deposits. However, quantities in most other artifact categories also are small, the only exceptions being metates and manos and certain types of flaked stone artifacts. Consequently, hunting was not necessarily any less important than most other subsistence pursuits.

Mammal bones identified to specific taxa are in low densities at SBA-931, and the diversity of taxa is lower than at SBA-539 and 670. Nearly all of the bone came from the upper stratum of Areas A and B, and what little bone was encountered in the lower stratum cannot be confidently associated with the earlier occupation because of the problem of rodent disturbance. In fact, the magnitude of rodent disturbance is reflected in the substantial number of pocket gopher bones. Out of the total of 432 bones identifiable to at least the family taxonomic level, 281 are of the California pocket gopher *(Thomomys bottae)*, these bones accounting for 35.8 percent of the total identified bone weight. A number of nearly complete gopher skeletons were encountered during excavation, an obvious indication of their dying in their burrows.

Discounting the gopher bones, rabbits and jackrabbits account for 131 of the 151 identified bones and 35.7 percent of the identified bone weight. Only 9 identifiable deer bones are in the collection, but they account for 62.2 percent of the identified bone weight. Although no bones could be assigned to particular sea mammal

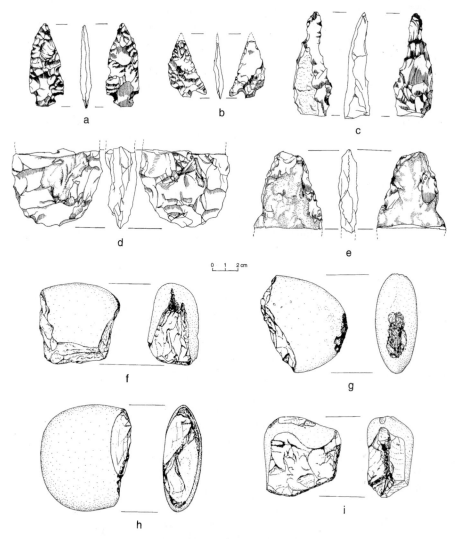

FIGURE 5.11   *Artifacts from SBA-931. a: corner-notched point similar to notched points found along Santa Barbara Channel dating to about 5000 B.P.; b: fragmentary contracting-stem point typical of the period approximately between 4500 B.P. and 1500 B.P.; c: narrow preform, perhaps intended to be a borer or drill before it broke; d–e: typical preforms; f–i: edge-ground flaked cobbles, some used also as hammerstones.*

taxa, sea mammal bone is present, and the dietary importance of sea mammals will be addressed in Chapter 7. In general, the assemblage of taxonomically identified bones resembles those from the two midden strata at SBA-670 in that it reflects the importance of rabbit and deer hunting.

An analysis of microwear on a sample of flake tools from SBA-931 revealed that the edges of 8 of the 33 exhibiting some form of microwear were used to cut meat. It is clear, then, that some butchering of meat took place on-site.

Nearly all of the bird bones in the SBA-931 collections are from the upper stratum of Areas A and B. Most of the taxa represented in the assemblage inhabit freshwater wetland habitats, which are still extensive below SBA-931 near the mouth of the Santa Ynez River. Ducks (most or all in the family Anatinae) account for 16 of the 24 bones identified at least to the family taxonomic level. Identified species in this family include teals and mallards *(Anas* spp.) and wigeons *(Mareca* spp.). Also represented by 1 or 2 bones are snow goose *(Chen hyperborea),* ruddy duck *(Oxyura jamaicensis),* and American coot *(Fulica americana).* Significantly, no cormorants, which were so well represented in the SBA-539 and 670 assemblages, are present, perhaps because the freshwater birds inhabiting the lagoon at the mouth of the Santa Ynez River were so much more accessible.

Taxa represented by the fish remains from SBA-931 are mostly those seen in the fish remains from SBA-539 and 670. Again, essentially all fish remains are from the upper stratum of Areas A and B. Compared to SBA-539 and 670, surfperches are proportionately more abundant at SBA-931, accounting for 30 of the 47 bones, whereas sardines and anchovies account for only 11 of the total. Hunting sea mammals may not have been as important to the occupants of SBA-931, so fewer sardine and anchovy bones might have come to the site as stomach contents.

A problem arises in attempting to determine the importance of shellfish collecting during each of the two principal occupations at SBA-931. In the discussion of the site chronology, I pointed out that most of the shellfish remains in the upper stratum probably were brought up by rodents from the lower stratum. As mentioned earlier, however, the variation in the radiocarbon dates probably indicates that some of the shell in the upper stratum probably is a product of shellfish collecting during the later occupation. Available data do not allow the amount of shell associated with the upper stratum to be estimated, although more than 90 percent probably is a product of shellfish collecting during the earlier occupation.

California mussel comprises 99.2 percent of the shellfish assemblage, and it is associated with small amounts of other taxa inhabiting the rocky intertidal zone. However, also present are sparing amounts of Venus clams *(Chione* spp.), piddocks *(Zirfaea pilsbryi* and *Barnea subtruncata),* and California oyster *(Ostrea lurida),* all taxa but the last living buried in tidal mudflats of an enclosed bay or estuary. Today the mouth of the Santa Ynez River does not have this type of habitat, but it probably did prior to construction of three dams along the river's middle and upper reaches. At any rate, such a habitat must have existed earlier than 5000 B.P., when SBA-931 was inhabited. The minor importance of the tidal mudflat habitat probably was a result of the relative difficulty of collecting shellfish that live buried in muds.

As was the case at SBA-539 and 670, milling implements are the only artifacts at SBA-931 indicative of plant foods. Metates and manos are in much greater densities at SBA-931 than at SBA-539 and 670, whereas mortars and pestles are quite rare. In the SBA-931 collections from Areas A and B are 52 complete or nearly complete manos, 46 small fragments of manos, and 48 metate fragments. In contrast, the collections from Areas A and B contain only two nearly complete globular mortars and two mortar fragments. Probably all milling artifacts are associated with the later occupations at SBA-931; none are clearly from the lower stratum.

Grasslands, where seed collecting probably occurred, exist today near SBA-931, and they may have been more extensive prior to agricultural use of the lands earlier in this century. Seeds and other edible plant parts also may have been collected from marshlands adjacent to the Santa Ynez River. However, habitats from which small seeds might have been gathered also exist in the vicinity of SBA-539 and 670, so the emphasis on seed collecting at SBA-931 probably is related to a subsistence focus prevalent at the time SBA-931 was inhabited rather than to greater local abundances of seed-bearing plants.

The Settlement Contexts of SBA-931

The diversity of artifact categories in the SBA-931 collections indicates that the site was a residential base during the later of the two principal occupations. However, SBA-931 differs from SBA-539 and 670 in containing generally low densities of artifacts and other cultural remains. Only metates and manos and certain classes of flaked stone tools are in relatively high densities. The generally low artifact densities indicate that occupation either was for short periods during an annual cycle of mobility between sites, but recurring many times, or for relatively long periods, but recurring very few times. The latter possibility is supported by data obtained from the 4 m×12 m area excavation. The artifacts whose three-dimensional positions were plotted occurred in three loose areal clusters, each of which may be largely the product of an occupation by a distinct family group. Of course, the occupations represented by the three clusters may not have been contemporaneous, that is, each cluster may represent a distinct occupation of Area A as well as an occupation by a distinct family group. It seems clear, nonetheless, that Area A was not occupied very many times. If it had, areal clusters of artifacts created by individual occupations would become blurred as locations of encampment shifted somewhat with each successive occupation.

Artifacts indicative of use as a residential base during the later occupation include many of same categories found at SBA-539 and 670. For instance, ten tarring pebbles and 4 g of asphaltum indicate waterproofing of basketry water containers. In contrast, the SBA-931 collections contain many more core hammerstones—32 in all. These undoubtedly were used to shape metates and manos and to pit their working surfaces periodically to maintain milling efficiency.

There are 100 biface preforms in the collections from Areas A and B (Figure 5.11), but, as was the case at SBA-670, waste flake characteristics indicate that preforms were preliminarily formed at another location, probably near a chert source. As well, reduction of preforms into finished tools was not typically undertaken at SBA-931. An unusually high percentage (14 percent) are narrower than those found at other Vandenberg sites. Arnold suspects that these narrow preforms were manufactured into some sort of macrodrill or borer, although no such artifacts are present in the SBA-931 assemblage. Macrodrills are present in many Vandenberg collections, as well as collections from sites in neighboring regions, but most I have seen are trifacial, implying a different manufacturing trajectory than that implied by these preforms. The type of tool made from the narrow preforms of SBA-931, and the location of its use, remain unknown.

Relative to SBA-539 and 670, knapping activity at SBA-931 concentrated more on production of flake tools from cores, there being 90 cores in the Areas A and B collections. While some flakes are perhaps simply waste from manufacture of core hammerstones, others obviously are tools. Indeed, there are 224 utilized or retouched flakes in the collections, and the 33 with evidence of microwear include 25 that were used for a wide variety of manufacturing and maintenance tasks. Ten of the tools were used to cut, scrape, or saw wood; seven were used to cut plant material; six were used to cut, saw, or drill bone or antler; and two were used to work hide.

Also relatively abundant are edge-ground flaked cobbles, there being 57 from Areas A and B (Figure 5.11). These tools are cobbles of fine-grained quartzite that have been bifacially flaked to form one or more relatively blunt and irregular edges. The prominences along these edges are slightly faceted by abrasion against a hard surface, presumably an abrasive rock such as sandstone. My experiments with replications of these artifacts indicate that they could have been used to scrape pulp from fibrous plant stems or leaves by placing the stems or leaves on a flat sandstone surface (a metate?) and drawing the flaked edge along the stem while pressing down.

The lack of artifacts attributable to the earliest occupation at SBA-931 indicates that it probably did not serve as a residential base during the earliest period of occupation, around 8300 B.P.–9000 B.P. Indeed the focus of activity appears to have been on collection and consumption of shellfish. Hunting and fishing, although probably practiced, were clearly minor subsistence pursuits by comparison. The lack of organic content in the lower stratum soil indicates that occupation probably did not entail much use of fire in food preparation. In Area A the lower stratum is only about 10 cm–15 cm thick, which implies that occupation entailed either many very short periods, perhaps only a few days in length, or relatively few longer periods as much as several weeks long. The latter seems more likely given that shellfish remains are reasonably well preserved. If occupations were only a few days every several months, the shells would have become quite weathered between occupations.

Little can be said about the social composition of the group or groups occupying the site around 8300 B.P.–9000 B.P. One possibility is that females were the principal occupants, since shellfish gathering is frequently a female activity. It seems equally possible, however, that relatively mobile groups of male hunters occupied the site and depended on shellfish when game was not readily available. Complete family groups are just as likely to have been the site occupants. Whatever the social composition was, the number of people occupying the site at any one time undoubtedly was quite small. The areal extent of the lower stratum in Area A is perhaps no more than 20 m or 30 m in diameter, and in Area B it was even smaller. This suggests that no more than 10 or 15 people occupied the site.

Activities typical of both sexes are represented by the cultural remains associated with the later occupation. Milling with metates and manos probably was a female activity, whereas biface reduction probably was a male activity. Assuming these associations, complete family groups must have occupied the site during the later period. The number of people occupying the site at any one time probably was relatively small. Considering that the area of relatively high densities of cultural remains is only about 30 m to 50 m in diameter in Area A and about 20 m in diameter in Area B, site occupants probably numbered no more than 20 individuals.

SBA-931 was in an ideal location for exploiting resources in the marshlands along the lower reaches of the Santa Ynez River as well as the estuary or ponds at the mouth of the river. These habitats would have existed during all periods of occupation, although their extents and locations surely were quite different during the earliest occupation about 8300 B.P.–9000 B.P. At this time sea level was 15 m to 30 m lower than it is now, so the marshlands directly below SBA-931 also would have been 15 m to 30 m lower, given that the gradient of the lower Santa Ynez River would have been adjusted to sea level at that time. Since the shoreline was 1.4 km to 3.8 km farther west at that time, an estuary and tidal flats would have been that much farther west too.

The locations of shellfish beds also may have been farther west at 8300 B.P.–9000 B.P. Today, one must walk about 3 km northwest of SBA-931 to collect mussels from the rocky intertidal zone on the lee side of Purisima Point. This probably also was the situation during the later of the two principal occupations of SBA-931. Irregular contour lines on a bathymetric chart of nearshore waters imply that a submerged rocky shoreline exists about 1.4 km offshore immediately north of the mouth of the Santa Ynez River. If this currently submerged location was an intertidal zone supporting mussel beds at 8300 B.P.–9000 B.P., the distance one needed to walk to acquire mussels may have been no more than the current 3-km walk to the Purisima Point vicinity.

A recent study of fossil pollen from alluvial sediments at a locality a few kilometers northeast of SBA-931 (discussed in Chapter 6) revealed that the composition of plant communities in the vicinity of SBA-931 probably was not too different 8300 B.P.–9000 B.P. or during later periods of prehistory (Woodman et al. 1991). Grasslands and scrublands may have had different extents due to climatic fluctuation, but they probably were of approximately equal access throughout prehistory. Assuming this, deer and rabbit would have been relatively abundant during all periods of site occupation.

Because of the very exposed location of SBA-931, one would expect that occupation occurred during the mild-weather months from late spring through fall. Dependence on seeds, most of which reach maturity during the summer months, supports this presumption. Nonetheless, the presence of bones of the northern fulmer, snow goose, and green-winged teal indicate occupation during winter months, when these birds are present along the central and southern California coast. It is possible, of course, that the site was occupied for brief periods during virtually any season of the year when local resources were available.

SITES TESTED IN 1974

The 8 sites included in this study out of the 31 tested in 1974 are those with relatively large collections and either radiocarbon dates or shell bead cross-dates. However, the available data from each of these 8 sites is much less than those from SBA-539, 670, and 931, and because most excavated deposits from the 1.5 m×1.5 m units were passed through fourth-inch mesh screens rather than eighth-inch mesh, the data from these sites are not always comparable to those from the 3 sites discussed so far. Nonetheless, the addition of the data from these 8 sites, particularly those data from column samples that were screened through eighth-inch mesh, makes it possible to address many of the research problems that would not have been possible had the analysis depended on data from only the 3 sites excavated in 1978–80.

Although some of the collections from these sites are quite small, I believe all served as residential bases, even though durations of occupation during an annual cycle probably varied considerably from site to site. The basis for this inference is that even the small collections contain artifacts normally associated with a commitment to stay at the site for more than a few days. All of the sites, for instance, contain some quantities of asphaltum, indicative of a variety of manufacturing and maintenance activities (see earlier discussion of SBA-539). More importantly, all sites have relatively dense midden deposits in which faunal remains are moderately to very dense, and all soil matrices are gray-brown in color due to the accumulation of charcoal and soot from fires and other organic remains. In addition, midden constituents are well preserved, as would be expected if occupation was long enough for midden to accumulate relatively rapidly.

SBA-210, West Side of Agua Vina Creek

SBA-210 along with its immediate neighbor on the opposite side of perennial Agua Vina Creek, SBA-552, are located at the base of Tranquillon Ridge, which overlooks the south-facing coastline along the southern margin of Vandenberg. Compared to all other sites included in this analysis, the geographic position of SBA-210 and 552 afforded considerably more protection from prevailing winds from the northwest and cool, damp fogs. This is undoubtedly an important reason why both sites are among the largest in terms of volume of deposits in the Vandenberg region. Indeed, few other sites in southern California contain midden deposits as deep as those at SBA-210 and 552.

One of the six units excavated at SBA-210 reached a depth of 5.6 m before sterile deposits were encountered, and four of the others reached depths between 1.6 m and 4.2 m (Figure 5.12). Shoring of the 1.5 m×1.5 m units with plywood sheets held in place with expansion jacks was necessary to reach depths in excess of 2 meters. Although the site covers an area somewhat over 19 ha in size, the area of deposits in excess of 2 m deep is much less, probably no more than 2.2 ha in area. The volume of excavated deposits was 41.85 m³.

A total of 126 glass trade beads in the collections verifies that SBA-210 was the Chumash village of *Nocto*. When the Portolá expedition of 1769–70 visited Nocto, it was a settlement of ten thatched houses and 60 to 70 residents. Radiocarbon dates indicate that occupation of the site began more than 4,000 years ago. The following four dates were obtained from the unit with a maximum depth of 5.6 m:

^{14}C yrs B.P.	Corrected Date B.P.	Depth (cm)	Material Dated
2240±150	2045	180–200	California mussel and red abalone shell fragments
3530±200	3335	340–360	California mussel shell fragments
4320±200	4125	520–540	California mussel shell fragments
4650±230	4455	520–540	Red abalone shell

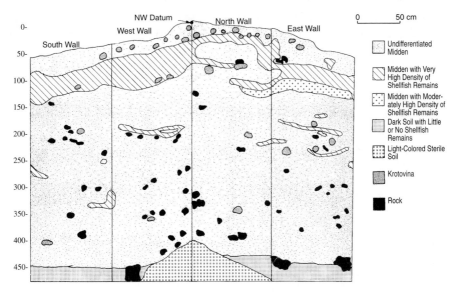

FIGURE 5.12   *Sidewall profile of an excavation unit at SBA-210.*

Considering the span of time between the earliest date and the historic period, as well as the area and depth of the cultural deposits, four radiocarbon dates are far too few for characterizing the site's depositional history. In lieu of an adequate number of dates, I used shell bead cross-dates to assign depth intervals in each unit to the major time periods used in the analysis. In the deeper parts of the site, test units revealed that the Terminal Early Period and the Middle Period each are represented by deposits 1 m to more than 2 m in depth, whereas the Late Period deposits generally are only in the upper 0.6 m. Once depth intervals of each unit were assigned to time periods, I was able to divide the collections accordingly.

SBA-210 yielded an assemblage of artifacts and other cultural remains substantially larger and more diverse than any of the other site assemblages obtained in 1974 or from any of the three sites investigated in 1978–80. The ethnohistorical documentation of the Chumash village of Nocto indicates that the site served as the only principal residential base on South Vandenberg (south of the Santa Ynez River valley) at the time of European contact. There seems little question that this role as the main residential base in the South Vandenberg region must have had a long prehistory. In part, the relatively high rate of accumulation of cultural remains expectable of a principal residential base accounts for the great depth of deposits, but because the site is at the base of a hill, soil deposition as a result of sheetwash off the hillside also steadily contributed to the depth of deposits.

SBA-552, East Side of Agua Vina Creek

SBA-552 has cultural deposits nearly as deep as those at SBA-210, the maximum depth reached in one of the three 1.5 m×1.5 m units excavated being 5.2 m. The site covers nearly twice the area of SBA-210, but the area of deposits exceeding 2 m in depth probably is only about 2 ha, or about the same size of the area of deep deposits at SBA-210. SBA-552 also contains relatively high densities of artifacts and other cultural remains, but a much smaller volume of deposits was excavated—a total of 20.03 m³. Moreover, the majority of the deposits in the areas investigated date earlier than 6500 B.P., when artifact assemblages typically were much less diverse in central and southern California.

Six radiocarbon dates exist for SBA-552. All but the first listed below came from the deepest of the three units.

¹⁴C yrs B.P.	Corrected Date B.P.	Depth (cm)	Material Dated
3630±200	3630	140–160	Wood charcoal
7140±90	6945	140–160	California mussel shell fragments
6910±280	6715	160–180	California mussel shell fragments
6700±120	6505	180–200	Barnacle and scaled worm-snail shell fragments
7580±300	7580	260–280	Wood charcoal
7990±350	7795	500–520	California mussel shell fragments

The second through the fourth dates listed above are in reverse stratigraphic order, although within a few hundred years of each other. This reversal probably is the result of mixing of deposits of somewhat different ages, an interpretation supported by the patchy nature of strata encountered between 140 cm and 180 cm in depth (Figure 5.13). Regardless of this problem, it is evident that deposits below about 120 cm from the surface of this unit date in excess of 6700 B.P. No other site in California is known to have deposits 4 m thick dating to such an early period of prehistory.

Because shell beads and other time-sensitive artifacts are not abundant in the SBA-552 collections, I had difficulty assigning depth intervals within each of the three units to time periods. The deposits below about 150 cm in the deepest unit were the only ones certainly dating to the Initial Early Period. The Terminal Early Period was represented by the lowermost deposits in two of the other units, but no clear distinction could be made between the Terminal Early and Middle Periods in the intermediate depths of all three units. The Late Period, however, was clearly represented in the upper 60 cm to 80 cm of deposits in two of the units. The absence of glass trade beads in the SBA-552 collection indicates that the site probably was not part of the village of Nocto at the time of European contact, although a few of the shell beads are of types in use just before contact.

As is the case with SBA-210 across Agua Vina Creek, SBA-552 contains unusually high densities of artifacts, particularly in those deposits dating after around 6700 B.P. For much of their prehistory SBA-552 and 210 probably were essentially one community, although the focus of settlement may have shifted back and forth between the two sites. However, it appears that only SBA-552 contains deposits dating to the Initial Early Period. The deposits dating to this period, the lower 4 m of the 5.2-m-deep unit, contain much lower densities of most classes of artifacts, milling implements being the major exception. Twenty-eight metate fragments, 15 typeable manos, and 10 small mano fragments came from these deposits (Figure 5.10). In contrast, chert biface preforms are absent, and chert waste flakes are

whereas the distinct dunal topography and weak soil development just below the surfaces of the Intermediate dunes led him to propose that they formed sometime after 5000 B.P. On South Vandenberg, Intermediate dunes form a distinct strip extending from the seacliff inland about 300 to 500 meters along the coast from just south of the Santa Ynez River mouth to the mouth of Honda Canyon (see Figure 3.1), and they cover Old dunes.

Old and Intermediate dunes are a product of two distinct periods of dune formation, even though they have been intermittently active to the present. This is most obvious along the inland (downwind) edge of the strip of Intermediate dunes on South Vandenberg. The distinct hills of the Intermediate dunes end abruptly, and beyond them is the gently undulating surface of the Old dunes. The stratigraphic relationship between Old and Intermediate dunes is evident on the face of the deep road cut through site SBA-670. Near the base of the road cut, one can trace the surface of the Old dune formation that was buried beneath the Intermediate dunes as they advanced inland. This surface is easily identified because of nearly a meter of medium brown soil immediately below it. The brown color of this soil stratum is caused by soil formation processes that occurred before the soil was buried. The Intermediate dune sand above the buried soil surface is orange-tan in color, and soil development immediately below the surface of Intermediate dunes is slight.

As discussed in Chapter 5, the Old dune soil merges with the lower midden stratum, along the SBA-670 road cut. This midden probably was deposited on the Old dune surface and eventually became mixed with the natural soil. After the occupation that created the lower midden stratum ended, the Intermediate dune soil formed on top of it, eventually to a height of nearly 15 m above the midden.

Corrected radiocarbon dates from the lower midden stratum range between 3175 B.P. and 4585 B.P. The corrected dates from the midden capping the Intermediate dune hill and exposed at the very top of the road cut range between 335 B.P. and 490 B.P.. These sets of dates indicate that the Intermediate dunes at SBA-670 formed sometime between 500 B.P. and 3200 B.P., a far narrower bracket of time than Johnson was able to propose based solely on characteristics of dune topography and degree of soil development. Nonetheless, there was no clear evidence of when during this bracket of time the Intermediate dunes formed. In terms of archaeological time, the formation of the Intermediate dunes in the vicinity of SBA-670 must have occurred relatively rapidly, since there are no apparent soil horizons in the profile of Intermediate dunes exposed in the road cut, except for the weakly developed soil at the top. Organic-stained soils do require a good deal of time to develop, however, so it is possible that the bulk of the Intermediate dunes formed over a time interval as much as several hundred years long. Regardless of the length of time required for the Intermediate dunes to form, it must have been an environmental event of significant magnitude. I will discuss later what such an event might have been.

Johnson derived additional evidence of paleoenvironmental conditions from his study of soils at SBA-931, near the mouth of the Santa Ynez River. The lower of the two archaeological strata at this site also is buried under accumulations of dune sand, but this stratum is much older than the one at SBA-670. As discussed in Chapter 5, corrected radiocarbon dates pertaining to this stratum range between 7775 B.P. and 8955 B.P., with all but 1 of the 11 dates being earlier than 8200 B.P. The dune sand overlying the lower midden stratum is approximately a meter thick, but confusing matters is the presence of cultural remains associated with a later occupation in this overlying sand. Johnson found no evidence of soil development in or directly below the buried archaeological stratum, implying that people who first occupied the site around 9000 B.P. deposited their discarded mussel shells on a surface that had only recently formed. However, Johnson was not able to determine the origin of this surface or of the unconsolidated sand immediately below it. The unconsolidated sand appears to have had at least a partial fluvial origin, based on the presence of small, waterworn pebbles, but wind deposition probably also was involved. Regardless of origin, the lack of soil development on the exposed, well-drained landform on which people discarded mussels 8,200 to 9,000 years ago implies some degree of environmental instability. For instance, at this time the landform may have been undergoing relatively rapid erosion or may have been subject to deposition of windblown sand. Unfortunately, we have no data for evaluating these or other possibilities.

The windblown sands on top of the 8,200- to 9,000-year-old stratum at SBA-931 are undated. Soil development in these sands immediately beyond the boundary of SBA-931 resembles that of Old dune deposits elsewhere on South Vandenberg, implying that at least some of the Old dune sands may have accumulated, or perhaps were redeposited, sometime after 9000 B.P. More than likely much of this sand layer was in place when people again occupied SBA-931 a few thousand years later. Although I was unable to obtain radiocarbon dates that are unquestionably associated with this later occupation, the artifact assemblage, which contains high proportions of metates and manos and lacks distinctive projectile point forms, implies a date of 5000 B.P. or earlier (see discussion of SBA-931 in Chapter 5).

Summarizing the evidence of paleoenvironmental change derived from Johnson's studies of soils and geomorphology, several events have been discerned:

1. Some type of environmental instability existed about 9000 B.P. that created ground surfaces lacking soil development in such locations as SBA-931.
2. Sometime between 8200 B.P. and 5000 B.P. Old dune sand accumulated in such locations as SBA-931, perhaps through redeposition from upwind locations. It is not clear, however, whether this accumulation was episodic; it could have been very gradual and may still be occurring to some extent. Significantly, however, it must postdate the first occupation of SBA-931, dating 8200 B.P.–9000 B.P., and it represents a change in environmental conditions favoring not only the accumulation of sand but also soil development.
3. Sometime between 3200 B.P. and 500 B.P. Intermediate dunes formed, and the lack of horizons of soil development within the Intermediate dunes implies that their formation was episodic. Although Johnson hesitates to propose a reason for the episode of dune activity, a period of aridity that reduced the kind of vegetation that stabilizes dune surfaces today is a likely possibility.
4. Intermediate dunes eventually became relatively stabilized, and soil development began to occur. This probably happened sometime before 500 B.P., when the latest occupation at SBA-670 began. Stabilization of dune surfaces and soil development would be expected to occur under environmental conditions similar to those of today.

A particularly important source of paleoenvironmental information is a sediment core obtained by oceanographers from the deepest part of the Santa Barbara Channel. The sediments from which the core was extracted are varved; that is, they are composed of thin layers of sediments rhythmically varying in grain size. A pair of these layers is called a varve and is the product of one year's deposition. To establish a chronology for the core the analysts simply counted varves, although they had to estimate the number of years represented by a series of bands of unvarved sediments. Consequently, the paleoenvironmental records derived from the core contents are tied to a high-resolution chronology extending back about 12,000 years, that is, through the whole Holocene epoch and back into the late Pleistocene epoch. This chronology is in *calendar* years, however, rather than *radiocarbon* years. As discussed in Chapter 4, radiocarbon years generally are longer than calendar years. To avoid confusion, I have converted the calendar years of the core's chronology to approximate radiocarbon years.

Palynologist Linda Heusser analyzed the fossil pollen preserved in the core in order to reconstruct a history of vegetational changes over the last 12,000 calendar years (Heusser 1978). The resulting reconstruction refers to a relatively large region because the pollen came to be deposited in the sediments of the core from the whole Santa Barbara Channel region, including the flanks of the Santa Ynez Mountains overlooking the channel. Although some pollen in the core may have come from the Vandenberg region, the amounts probably are negligible. Consequently, the vegetational changes based on the fossil pollen analysis probably are not the same as those that occurred in the Vandenberg region, although there may be some similarities. Here is a summary of the major vegetational changes reflected in the fossil pollen:

1. Prior to ca. 7000 B.P. (in radiocarbon years) pines *(Pinus* spp.) were much more extensive than they were thereafter. As well, ferns (Filicae) were more prevalent. These plant species reflect a cooler and wetter climate than is currently the case. Vegetation and climate still retained many characteristics typical of the late Pleistocene.
2. Between 7000 B.P. and 4900 B.P. pines decreased in abundance to their current extent. Oaks *(Quercus* spp.) became increasingly more prevalent and in fact were somewhat more prevalent that they are today. Climate was becoming warmer and probably drier, although how much warmer and drier is difficult to infer.
3. Between ca. 4900 B.P. and 2200 B.P. plants in the sunflower family (Asteraceae) became particularly abundant relative to other plant taxa represented by the pollen. However, the proportions of different pollen taxa fluctuated through this period, implying relatively unstable climatic conditions. Heusser believes that this was a period of relatively open habitats and warmer-than-present climatic conditions.
4. After ca. 2200 B.P. various chaparral species became relatively more prevalent than before. Heusser suspects that climate may have become cooler and wetter during this period, reaching current conditions. However, she proposes that the increase in chaparral species may be related to an increased prevalence of fire caused by human intervention. The Chumash at the time of European contact are known to have burned purposefully lands in the coastal plain in order to propagate certain seed-bearing plants of interest, but the history of this practice has not been documented archaeologically.

In addition to the relatively generalized record of vegetational change reflected in the Santa Barbara Channel pollen record, a pollen record recently has been extracted from alluvial sediments in two neighboring localities on Vandenberg not far north of the Santa Ynez Valley. Prepared for the firm SAIC in support of their archaeological project along a proposed oil pipeline route (Woodman et al. 1991), this record is broadly similar to the Santa Barbara Channel pollen record, but it also is different in many respects. The differences, of course, are a product of vegetational characteristics specific to the Vandenberg region, or even more specifically to the localities where the fossil pollen samples were obtained.

Unfortunately, there are problems with the dating of the pollen record. Two of the seven radiocarbon dates for one of the pollen profiles and two of the nine dates for the other are reversed stratigraphically, the amount of discrepancy ranging between 660 and 1,850 years. Because of the magnitude and high incidence of the reversals, accuracy of all the dates is called into question. I suspect that those dates accepted as stratigraphically consistent could be in error by as much as 500 to 1,000 years. Regardless of vagaries that may exist in dating the pollen record, the data are very important in providing an initial picture of vegetational and paleoenvironmental change within the Vandenberg region. The major vegetational changes revealed in this pollen record are as follows:

1. Between 11,000 B.P., when the record begins, to 4000 B.P. vegetation was open, consisting of grasses and species of the sunflower family. The predominant species in the sunflower family probably was coastal sage. Climatic conditions throughout this period are interpreted to have been warm and dry. There is no evidence of a prevalence of pines and wetland species prior to 7000 B.P., as seen in the Santa Barbara Channel record, even though bishop pines are quite abundant in a number of localities on Vandenberg today. The low incidence of pine pollen throughout the record may be a result of the lack of pines near the locations where the pollen cores were obtained.

2. After 4000 B.P. plants of the sunflower family decreased, and a wide variety of plant species with greater water requirements became more abundant. Pines also are more abundant than before. Climate is interpreted to have shifted to cooler and wetter conditions. This contrasts with the Santa Barbara Channel record, in which plant taxa indicative of warm, dry climatic conditions reached their peak between 4900 B.P. and 2200 B.P.

3. Between 1700 B.P. and 1100 B.P. plants of the sunflower family again increased, and, concomitantly, chaparral plants decreased. Climate during this period again was warm and dry. There is no comparable interval in the Santa Barbara Channel record. Instead, chaparral species and a cooler, wetter climate became more prevalent after 2200 B.P.

4. After 1100 B.P. chaparral species and oaks became significantly more abundant at the expense of plants in the sunflower family. Climate again shifted to cooler and wetter conditions. As mentioned, the Santa Barbara Channel record shows these conditions beginning around 2200 B.P.

In general, the Vandenberg pollen record does not reflect vegetational changes as profound as those seen in the Santa Barbara Channel record. In addition to the likelihood that vegetation communities in the immediate vicinity of the pollen cores responded to climatic changes conservatively, the strong maritime influence of the region's climate may have ameliorated the effects of climatic change. The Santa Barbara Channel pollen record is more influenced by vegetational changes occurring some distance inland, on the flanks of the Santa Ynez Mountains. Vegetational changes may have been more profound in these geographic situations than in a coastal region subject to strong prevailing winds from offshore.

Fossils of radiolaria, which are marine microorganisms, were preserved in the sediments of the same core from which palynologist Heusser extracted fossil pollen.

Oceanographer Niklas Pisias used variations in species of radiolaria to reconstruct fluctuations in near-surface sea water temperature during the last 8,000 calendar years (Pisias 1978; Figure 6.3). Since water temperature correlates with coastal air temperature, the record of sea temperature variations informs on an important aspect of climatic history. The major periods in Pisias's temperature record are as follows:

1. From the beginning of his reconstruction about 7000 B.P. to about 4700 B.P. (in radiocarbon years), sea water was generally very warm—warm enough, in fact, that kelp beds along the Santa Barbara Channel probably could not survive much of the time. If these warm temperatures prevailed along the Vandenberg coast, the productivity of mussel beds would have diminished.
2. Between around 4700 B.P. and 3600 B.P. water temperature was relatively cool, similar to current water temperatures.
3. Between 3600 B.P. and 3100 B.P. water temperature again was very warm. Again, kelp and mussel beds probably were adversely affected.
4. Between 3100 B.P. to 2000 B.P. temperatures again approximated current temperatures.
5. Between 2000 B.P. and 800 B.P. temperatures were relatively warm, although they did not reach the higher temperatures of the previous two warm-water periods.
6. After 800 B.P. channel waters cooled to their current temperature.

Few correlations may be discerned between Heusser's pollen record and Pisias's water temperature record, even though their data came from the same sediment core. The only obvious correlation is between the period during which pines decreased and oaks expanded, between 7000 B.P. and 4900 B.P., and a period of generally very warm sea water temperatures. However, climatic fluctuations typically are difficult to infer from variations in a pollen record. In contrast, there is a close and relatively direct relationship between the record of change in species of fossil radiolaria and water temperature changes.

It would be ideal to have an equally sensitive record of precipitation fluctuations so that periods of significant aridity could be identified. The only record of this sort covers the relatively short period from 1,600 calendar years ago to the present; it is based on the analysis of tree rings of old trees growing on San Gorgonio Peak, located about 350 km east of Vandenberg. Significantly, however, this record is long enough to provide some insights into the relationships between fluctuations in water temperature and precipitation. Pisias argued that significant periods of warm water temperatures were correlated with greater precipitation, implying that Santa Barbara Channel climate during the Holocene fluctuated between warm-wet and cool-dry climatic conditions. While there is some correlation of this sort since modern climatic records have been kept, the San Gorgonio Peak tree-ring record indicates that the relationship between temperature and precipitation is more complicated than Pisias presumed. In fact, an analysis by Dan Larson and Joel Michaelsen (n.d.) of the relationship between the water temperature and precipitation inferred from the San Gorgonio Peak tree-ring record revealed that increased precipitation correlated with periods of both warm and cool waters.

They argued, as I would, that periods of low productivity of food resources would be those during which water (and air) temperature was high and precipitation was low. During the 1,600-calendar-year period of the tree-ring record, their analysis revealed four periods when these conditions occurred: 1345–1375, 1245–1295,

Water Temperature (deg. C)

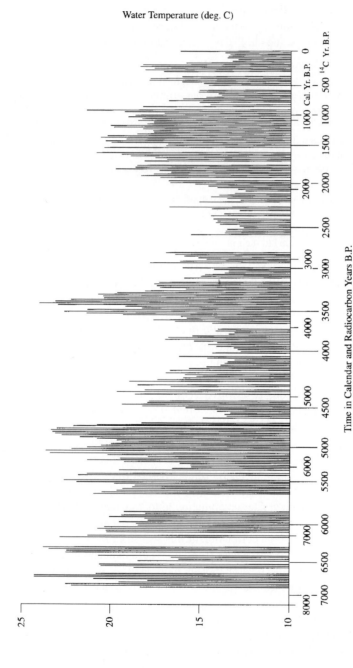

Time in Calendar and Radiocarbon Years B.P.

FIGURE 6.3 *Sea water paleotemperature record for the Santa Barbara Channel. Reconstructed by Niklas Pisias, this record is based on fluctuations in different species of fossil radiolaria found in a core of sediments from the bottom of the channel. The temperature values are spaced approximately 25 years apart except for gaps where sediments were not layered in varves. Using the CALIB computer program (Stuiver and Reimer 1993), I added radiocarbon dates approximately correlated to Pisias's calendar year time scale. In some instances, however, a radiocarbon date may be correlated with a calendar year time interval as much as 300 years long (such as a radiocarbon date of 2500±60 B.P. may be correlated with any of several different calendar dates between 2400 B.P. and 2710 B.P.).*

995–1015, and 795–875 calendar years B.P. These are all very short intervals of time compared to those of concern to us, but they do verify that high air/water temperatures can correlate with low precipitation to produce periods of significant aridity. Indeed, the period between 875 and 795 calendar years B.P. is of particular significance, as we shall see. The broader implication of their study is that even if precipitation fluctuations were largely independent of temperature variations, intervals of low precipitation occurring during periods when air/water temperatures were quite warm would have had devastating effects on terrestrial as well as intertidal resources.

How can these various paleoenvironmental records be reconciled, if indeed this is possible? Inevitably, some aspects of each record must be given less credence than others in any reconciliation, and a variety of criteria could be used in making such decisions. The synthesis I present below gives priority to the water paleotemperature record because it is closely related to a climatic variable: air temperature. I use the other paleoenvironmental records presented to infer fluctuations in precipitation and vegetation characteristics, but I consider these records to be less reliable because the links between the data upon which they are based and paleoenvironmental events are not as direct. I also refer to paleoenvironmental information from locations elsewhere in western North America, but only to show that some paleoenvironmental changes in the Vandenberg and neighboring regions affected much larger geographic areas. The paleoenvironmental reconstruction for the Vandenberg region is as follows:

1. Prior to 7000 B.P. climate likely was cooler than present. Because pines and ferns still were prevalent in the Santa Barbara Channel region, as they were during the Pleistocene epoch, annual precipitation levels may have been relatively high. However, vegetation communities in the Vandenberg region probably contained the same species they do today; only the geographic distribution of the communities was different. It is also possible that climatic conditions and vegetation communities were relatively unstable during portions of the period between about 12,000 B.P. and 7000 B.P., which may be the reason why the Vandenberg pollen record appears to indicate more arid climate and associated vegetation, and why soil development at SBA-931 was minimal around 9000 B.P.

2. Between 7000 B.P. and 4700 B.P. climate was significantly warmer than present. This is the period of the Altithermal in western North America, and a variety of evidence indicates that low precipitation levels accompanied the warm weather. Vegetation communities were becoming more open.

3. Between 4700 B.P. and about 2000 B.P. climate was generally cooler than before, but not always as cool as the present climate. Although the Santa Barbara Channel pollen record indicates that relatively warm and dry vegetation prevailed, the Vandenberg pollen record indicates that vegetation had shifted to types expectable during relatively cool and wet conditions but, again, not as cool and wet as today's climate.

4. The sharp increase in water temperature between around 3600 B.P. and 3100 B.P. has no obvious signature in either the Santa Barbara Channel or the Vandenberg pollen record, perhaps because these records cannot resolve climatic events of so short a duration. It is possible that this was a warm climatic interval only 200 or 300 years long. I suspect that precipitation levels were relatively low during at least part of this period, largely because this was likely the interval when the Intermediate dunes along the South Vandenberg coast (and likely elsewhere in the region) were most active.

5. Between about 2000 B.P. and 800 B.P. climate again became relatively warm, although generally not to the extremes of earlier periods such as the one just mentioned. Vegetation in the Vandenberg region became relatively open, which may reflect generally lower precipitation levels.

6. After 800 B.P. climate became generally cooler again, and distributions of vegetation communities approached today's, with chaparral becoming more prevalent. However, an 80-year period of very arid climatic conditions falls at the beginning of this period.

THE RELATIONSHIP BETWEEN POPULATION FLUCTUATIONS AND PALEOENVIRONMENTAL CHANGE

I stated in Chapter 3 that prehistoric hunter-gatherer populations did not necessarily respond to paleoenvironmental change just by expanding or reducing diet breadth to compensate for changes in food resource abundances. Instead, their numbers became larger or smaller as an adjustment to an increase or decrease in the abundance of food resources. If indeed there were relatively long periods of warm climate during which precipitation frequently was low, as the paleoenvironmental data seem to indicate, expansion of diet breadth during periods when essentially all food resources were becoming less abundant may not have been a successful response, especially during particularly bad years. As a consequence, population numbers would have declined. Conversely, if productivity of food resources increased, diet breadth very well may have decreased; at the same time, however, more reliable resources may have fostered increases in population numbers that kept diet breadth more or less the same. In light of these arguments, it makes sense to search for relationships between fluctuations in population density and paleoenvironmental changes affecting resource abundances. Once any such relationships have been discovered, or if they are suspected, the next step would be to determine how cultural change also may be implicated.

In the following assessment of relationships between changes in population density and paleoenvironmental change in the Vandenberg region, I consider whether time intervals characterized by relatively low frequencies of radiocarbon dated site components correlate with periods of relatively warm climate. Conversely, periods of cooler climate should be characterized by higher frequencies of components.

9000 B.P.–7400 B.P. (Paleocoastal Period extending into the Initial Early Period): Population appears to have been very low through this period, being particularly low prior to about 8400 B.P. There was noticeable growth between 8000 B.P and 7400 B.P., but following 7400 B.P. population appears to have declined. Although climate was apparently relatively cool and wet throughout this period, it would seem that the gradual growth of population beginning 8400 B.P–8000 B.P. may be related to the broad trend throughout North America of population growth following the demise of Paleoindian adaptations during the Pleistocene-Holocene transition. Alternatively, there may have been significant paleoenvironmental changes during this period that may account for an increase in population, particularly between 7800 B.P and 7400 B.P. Paleoenvironmental information for this period is just too sketchy even to suspect this was the case.

7400 B.P.–3600 B.P. (Initial Early Period extending into the Terminal Early Period): Population numbers appear to have remained relatively low throughout this period. Until about 4700 B.P. climate appears to have been relatively arid, which may account for the low population numbers at least until that date. The seemingly substantial population growth that took place after 5200 B.P. along the Santa Barbara Channel has no counterpart in the Vandenberg region. It is significant, however, that this interval of higher population numbers along the channel correlates nicely with a period of cooler climate.

3600 B.P. –3100 B.P. (Terminal Early Period/Middle Period transition): This period of quite warm weather correlates with the period of possibly lower population in the Vandenberg region, although evidence of lower population numbers during this time interval is much stronger along the Santa Barbara Channel. Radiocarbon date lists for a number of other regions of California show a distinct depression dating around 3000 B.P. that may be related to this same climatic event.

3100 B.P.–2000 B.P. (Initial portion of Middle Period): This period of seemingly favorable environmental conditions witnessed significant population growth in the Vandenberg region, although population appears to have fluctuated up and down.

2000 B.P.–1400 B.P. (Intermediate part of Middle Period): Weather remained relatively warm throughout this period, and there may have been intervals of significant dryness. Populations in both the Vandenberg and channel mainland regions declined during this period.

1400 B.P.–800 B.P. (Latter part of Middle Period): Population rose sharply during this period, but there was a decline between 1000 B.P. and 800 B.P. in both the Vandenberg and channel mainland regions. This decline seems to correlate with the period of very warm and dry weather occurring between 795 and 875 calendar years B.P.

800 B.P.–Contact (Late Period): Population in the Vandenberg region appears to have grown significantly during this period of generally cooler weather.

CONCLUSIONS

This assessment indicates that there is good reason for believing that environmental fluctuations had a significant impact on population growth. Although correlations are not perfect, there is a reasonably clear pattern of lower population density during periods of particularly warm weather. At least at times during these periods precipitation undoubtedly was low, creating particularly arid conditions when most kinds of food resources would have declined in productivity. Conversely, population density was higher during periods when climate was cooler. When precipitation was relatively high during these periods, food resources would have been more productive. However, after 2800 B.P. population density began to increase, albeit irregularly, to levels never before reached during earlier periods. Population growth is especially evident in the Vandenberg and the channel mainland after 1400 B.P. It would seem that after about 1400 B.P. populations living in the Vandenberg and neighboring regions developed adaptive means to compensate more effectively for declines in resource productivity. In the next chapter I shall evaluate whether there is evidence for such cultural developments.

In addition to the intervals of population growth late in prehistory, we should be concerned with earlier periods of population fluctuation—both growth and decline—that may correlate with cultural changes. Since the archaeological record currently is silent regarding events occurring during periods of population decline, it makes sense to assess what kinds of cultural development are apparent at times just after population density once again rose to high levels. I shall consider the evidence of such developments in the next chapter.

7

Confronting the Research Problems

INTRODUCTION

Having investigated the relationship between population and environment in the previous chapter, I now turn to the task of seeking evidence of changes in subsistence that might be a product of environmental shifts or population change or both. I argued in Chapter 3 that diet breadth, that is, the diversity of food resources exploited, was affected by either of two factors: (1) environmental changes that increased or decreased the abundance of resources or (2) population changes, particularly growth, which affected the per-capita availability of food resources. A complicating factor considered in the previous chapter is the prospect that population numbers after 1400 B.P. may have responded to decreases and increases in the abundance of food resources without any necessary change in diet breadth. One of the jobs ahead of me in this chapter, therefore, is to discover the circumstances favoring subsistence change other than, or in addition to, adjustment of population numbers to changing abundances of resources.

In addition, I shall consider how economic exchange enters into the picture, although data concerning economic exchange is not abundant and often provides an incomplete picture of economic relationships. I argued in Chapter 3 that the degree of participation in economic exchange may be related to population growth. Of particular interest is the extent to which chert projectile points, knives, or simply preforms were manufactured for export in an interregional exchange network. The relationship between biface preform production and imported trade items such as shell beads may give some insight into this question.

Before considering this set of research problems, however, it is necessary to delve into the nature of settlement systems on South Vandenberg. Specifically, I wish to consider in greater detail the place of those sites included in the analysis of settlement systems. I have argued that all of these sites are residential bases; however, undoubtedly there were many different kinds of residential bases used in South Vandenberg settlement systems. For instance, some residential bases may have been used for specialized food resource acquisition while others at which food acquisition was more generalized served as loci for initial reduction of biface preforms. If my objective is to elucidate subsistence change through time, I must control synchronic variability in subsistence practices among sites as much as possible.

Another reason for considering settlement contexts of sites is the possibility that patterns of mobility may have varied enough through time to have skewed significantly the frequency of sites per time period. Relatively more mobility during a particular time period may translate into more sites used by a population than would be the case if a population of the same size was relatively less mobile. In the previous chapter I mentioned that the impact of mobility changes on frequencies of site components per 200-year interval probably is relatively minor. Nonetheless, it makes sense to be sure this is the case. Indeed, because there is the possibility that greater mobility may have occurred during the Late Period, I shall give particular attention to Late Period settlement systems.

SETTLEMENT CONTEXTS OF THE SITES

Because all sites included in the analysis have relatively well-developed middens and contain artifacts associated with manufacture and maintenance activities, particularly those entailing relatively elaborate procedures such as tarring basketry water containers, I believe all sites served as residential bases occupied for weeks or months at a time. The presence of seed or acorn milling implements also strongly suggests use as a residential base, although it is conceivable that these implements were cached at a site for use during very brief visits. At sites where milling implements are relatively abundant, however, this possibility seems less likely.

In many parts of California and the Pacific Northwest ethnographically documented settlement systems are characterized by a winter residential base at which a group spent winter months as well as parts of the rest of the year subsisting primarily on stored food resources. During the warm months of the year, however, this group usually divided into relatively small kin units and occupied other residential bases for much shorter periods of time. Such residential bases, as well as camps where residence was very temporary, frequently were used only during a particular season when nearby resources of interest were abundant. Once the resources were depleted or out of season, the kin unit might move to another seasonally occupied residential base. However, while a winter residential base might have been regularly occupied from one year to the next, such regularity did not necessarily characterize occupation of summer residential bases and camps. Year-to-year variations in the distribution and abundance of food resources caused variations in settlement systems. For instance, a larger number of camps might have been used during unusually dry summers, when plant foods and game animals were more dispersed or in lower densities.

Ethnohistoric and ethnographic information concerning Chumash settlement systems is quite scanty, and most of it refers to the Santa Barbara Channel region. Some time ago, Lief Landberg (1965) delved into the problem of reconstructing Chumash settlement systems, and from a variety of ethnohistorical references to village abandonment and reoccupation he was able to infer that the Chumash typically remained in their principal villages during most of the winter and were dispersed much of the time from spring through fall. Along the Vandenberg coast, this type of settlement system probably was more complicated due to the availability of marine resources such as shellfish at many locations throughout the winter months. Even though winter weather along the coast is cool and windy, it certainly was not so inhospitable as to discourage winter occupation lasting at least several days at a time.

On the basis of what we know about Chumash settlement systems and those of other ethnographically or ethnohistorically documented aboriginal peoples along the Pacific coast, I would like to make a distinction between *principal* and *subsidiary* residential bases. The Chumash village of Nocto at the time of European contact would have been a principal residential base (see discussion of SBA-210 in Chapter 5). A subsidiary residential base would have been a site where a kin unit most likely containing one or several related families lived for a time as short as several days or as long as a few months. Unfortunately, we have identified no ethnographically or ethnohistorically documented subsidiary residential bases in the Vandenberg region to serve as examples, so the distinction between principal and subsidiary residential bases must rest solely on archaeological data.

Principal residential bases should contain a greater diversity of artifact categories than subsidiary residential bases under the assumption that a broader range of activities took place at principal residential bases. For instance, because subsistence depended not only on immediately available foods but also stored foods brought to the residential base, food processing activities should be more diverse than they would be at subsidiary residential bases, where dependence on seasonally and locally available resources would have been more the rule. Similarly, winter occupation at principal residential bases would have been the most appropriate time for manufacture and repair of tools and facilities used during the warm months of the year, when efforts were concentrated more on the food quest. Principal residential bases also would be the locations where most ritual and other social events took place, some of which no doubt were associated with artifacts that eventually would become part of the archaeological record.

Table 7.1 summarizes information concerning artifact diversity from the different site components included in the analysis. I have tabulated in this table not only the size of each artifact collection but also the number of artifact categories into which I classified the artifacts. I also divided excavated volumes and collections with respect to any period divisions I was able to recognize.

Archaeologists have recognized that studies of artifact diversity must compensate for the effects of sample size, that is, the number of artifacts in a collection (Conkey 1980; Kintigh 1984). In other words, one would expect that diversity would increase as the size of the collection increases. This correlation exists because the larger a collection is, the greater the probability that rare artifact types will be present. To deal with this problem, which is significant in the case of the Vandenberg collections, I produced Figure 7.1, which is a plot of the number of artifacts against the number of artifact categories in the collection from each site component listed in Table 7.1. My initial plot revealed that the number of artifact categories increased at a lower rate than the increase in the number of artifacts in the collection. This kind of relationship is expectable because the larger an artifact collection is, the more likely it will contain virtually all the artifact categories represented in the total number of artifacts present in a site's deposits. In short, there is an exponential relationship between these two variables.

TABLE 7.1
EXCAVATED VOLUME, COLLECTION SIZE, AND NUMBER OF ARTIFACT CATEGORIES

Site SBA-	Excavated Volume in cu. m	No. of Artifacts in Collection.[1]	No. of Artifact Categories
539	16.4	366	48
670, Upper Stratum	44.9	42	21
670, Lower Stratum	7.7	164	21
931, Area A	93.5	567	59
210, Terminal Early Period Levels	12.6	392	65
210, Middle Period Levels	22.5	664	71
210, Late Period Levels	6.8	230	51
552, Initial Early Period Levels	8.8	145	48
552, Terminal Early/Middle Period Levels	8.1	124	44
552, Late Period Levels	3.2	87	41
530	3.0	3	4
551, Eastern Sector	9.5	13	14
551, Western Sector	4.1	12	9
662	21.3	72	28
663	3.6	2	3
690	4.0	4	5
1040	10.1	13	13

[1]Excludes artifacts whose abundance is expressed as weights.

Given the exponential relationship between number of artifacts and number of artifact categories, I converted the former to a log scale so a straight regression line (as opposed to one that is curved) could express relationship between the two variables. The regression line drawn through the points in the plot shown in Figure 7.1 is, in a sense, the average trend represented by all the points on the plot. Points that depart from the line to the lower right represent sites tending to have less diversity of artifact categories than would be expected on the basis of sample size, whereas points that depart from the line to the upper left represent sites tending to have higher diversity than would be expected on the basis of sample size. Sites close to or on the line do not show a clear pattern one way or the other. To gain some idea of the degree of confidence one may have in the degree of diversity, I drew what are called confidence lines on either side of the regression line. Points falling beyond the confidence lines have a 90-percent chance of being significantly more or less diverse.

Only the points representing the collections from the Terminal Early Period and Middle Period components of SBA-210 are beyond the upper confidence line, indicating significant diversity beyond the 90-percent confidence level. Moreover, the Initial Early Period and Late Period components of SBA-552 are practically on the upper 90-percent confidence line, and the remaining components at SBA-210 and 552 at least are above the regression line. This pattern indicates that these two sites tend to have greater diversities of artifact categories represented in their collections during all major periods of occupation. It appears that these two neighboring sites, taken together, served as a principal residential base through nearly 8,000 years of prehistory and continued as such when the Chumash village of Nocto existed at SBA-210 at the time of European contact.

Three site components, SBA-662 and the upper and lower strata of SBA-670, contain lower artifact category diversities than would be expected on the basis of sample size. In the case of the lower stratum of SBA-670, this is the result of an unusually large number of biface preforms inflating the total number of artifacts in the collection. Similarly, unusually large numbers of point fragments, chert cores, and utilized flakes have inflated SBA-662's artifact total. That is, special emphases on reduction of biface preforms at SBA-670 and the production and use of flake tools at SBA-662 created the relatively low artifact diversities at this site. This explanation does not work so well with regard to the upper stratum of SBA-670, where relatively large numbers of utilized flakes and beads have skewed the artifact total. The marginal position of all the excavation units except those excavated in 1974 may have created this distinctive pattern in artifact frequencies.

Intersite variations in artifact diversity, and the emphases on particular activities at certain sites such as SBA-662 and 670, reveal that with more and higher-quality data than is currently available it should be possible to divide subsidiary residential

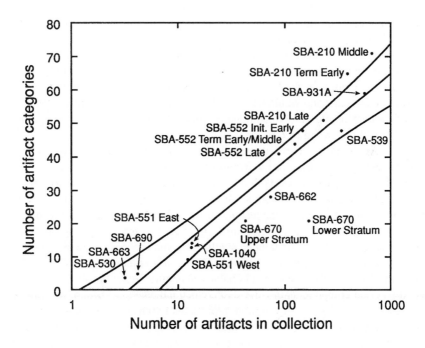

FIGURE 7.1 *Diversity of artifact categories in relation to collection size. The curved lines above and below the straight regression line delimit the 90-percent confidence interval.*

bases into a number of different types. Information on season or seasons of occupation also would be very helpful in such an endeavor.

One should also keep in mind that other major types of sites exist on South Vandenberg. Although not among the sites included in this analysis, a number of sites probably are not residential bases of any sort. These sites generally lack midden deposits, but they often do contain moderate densities of flaked stone and scatters of shell fragments. These sites appear to have served as camps used for very brief periods, perhaps only for a few hours while an animal was butchered and a meal or two consumed. Research I directed near the northern extreme of Vandenberg Air Force Base, in a geographic locality known as the San Antonio Terrace, contained many such sites (Chambers Consultants and Planners 1984). The terrace is covered with stabilized dunes of Intermediate age, and small wetlands exist between dune ridges that attract deer and probably other game animals. The sites among these dunes contain no midden deposits to speak of, and their artifacts appear to have been related primarily to hunting and butchering. Although residential bases exist on the margins of the dunes, none has been located within the dunes.

Another indicator of a site's role as a residential base is the rate at which cultural remains accumulated. A site serving as a principal residential base would be expected to have a high rate of accumulation due to the longer period during an annual cycle when the site was occupied, and perhaps also due to a greater intensity of midden-producing activities. Ideally, a measurement of the rate of accumulation of cultural remains would be the quantities that accumulated per unit of time. Given that an excavation unit is a vertical, parallel-sided column through a site's deposits and that radiocarbon dates or precise artifact cross-dates allow depth intervals to be translated into time intervals, the quantities of cultural remains per time interval could be calculated. The problem with the Vandenberg data, however, is that detailed chronologies for sites do not exist and would be difficult to create even if an infinite number of radiocarbon dates could be obtained due to mixing of deposits by burrowing animals and other soil-disturbing factors.

As an alternative, I use densities of certain classes of cultural remains per unit volume of deposits without reference to the amount of time represented by the deposits. This alternative assumes that noncultural accumulation of soil does not vary significantly from one site to another. If it did, there would be no way to avoid using the more sophisticated approach just outlined. Table 7.2 presents the frequencies and densities of categories of common artifacts related to manufacturing and maintenance activities. I have also included shellfish remains because they are a product of a nearly ubiquitous subsistence activity. The several components of SBA-210 and 552 stand out from the other sites in having generally higher densities of most artifact categories as well as flakes and shell, which indicate that cultural remains accumulated at these two sites much more rapidly than at the other sites included in the study. Occupants of these two sites must have lived at these sites for significantly longer periods during an annual cycle than they did at other South Vandenberg sites.

That the site complex consisting of SBA-210 and 552 served as a principal residential base throughout prehistory is not surprising if one considers its favorable environmental setting. As I described in Chapter 5, SBA-210 and 552 are protected from the full brunt of prevailing winds from the northwest by a high ridge, and a seen on the San Antonio Terrace on North Vandenberg. Bamforth's (1986) study of flaked stone collections from Terrace sites, along with my analysis of other cultural remains (Chambers Consultants and Planners 1984), reveals a clear pattern of increasing differentiation among site types from the Middle to Late Period.

Turning back to the original question, why Late Period population increased to much higher levels than previously, two possible explanations are worth considering. One possible explanation is that continual development of new subsistence technology or improvements to existing technology allowed population to grow in spite of environmental perturbations. By the beginning of the Late Period a variety of different subsistence technologies were in place that facilitated expansion of diet breadth. First, acorn processing technology had been developed a few thousand years earlier. Second, hook-and-line fishing appears to have been made more efficient with the introduction of the circular shell fishhook around 2000 B.P.–2500 B.P., and near the beginning of the Late Period there was an improved shank shape for attachment of line to the fishhook. Third, the bow and arrow came into use about 1500 B.P. One could argue that these technological developments allowed populations of the Vandenberg region to withstand more effectively hard times brought about by periods of lowered food resource productivity. This explanation certainly is plausible, but we do not yet understand well enough the efficiencies of different subsistence technologies to have much confidence in it.

The alternative explanation has to do with the development of regional and interregional economic systems. Production of olivella shell beads in the Santa Barbara Channel region began to increase during the latter part of the Middle Period, about 800 B.P.–1000 B.P., and near the beginning of the Late Period a few hundred years later the olivella callus bead, used as money at the time of European contact, came into existence. Sometime later during the Late Period production of olivella money beads, and probably other types of olivella beads, increased dramatically (Arnold 1992b). The increased production and use of olivella beads reflects an important development of the regional economic systems among the Late Period occupants of the Vandenberg region and neighboring regions. As Chester King describes, the occupants of one Chumash village could sell to occupants of a neighboring village surplus food resources available during a specific season of the year. The shell beads obtained from this sale later could be used to acquire resources available during a different season from the same or another village (King 1971:31). Moreover, a group could manufacture items for which there was a demand, sell these products in exchange for shell beads, and then used accumulated shell beads to purchase food during a lean season or year.

The intensification of monetized exchange between Chumash villages occurring around 700 B.P.–800 B.P. as a response to instability in food resource availability brought about by a period of warm climatic conditions was Jeanne Arnold's argument, which I discussed in Chapter 2. She proposed that strong political leaders who arose at this time controlled much of the intervillage exchange. If indeed shell-bead money facilitated the flow of food resources to localities when they were needed to compensate for local deficiencies, it makes sense that the intensification of money-based exchange would have occurred during a period when there was increased frequency of local shortfalls in the availability of food resources. With this intensified monetary system in place after environmental conditions improved, it would have facilitated growth of population to higher levels than would have been possible prior to the development of the exchange system. This is because population size would not have been so closely checked by environmental fluctuations.

Of course, both elaboration of subsistence technology and intensification of money-based exchange could have played a role and no doubt did. It is well to keep in mind, however, that the growth of population in the Vandenberg region may have been largely a result of technological and economic developments in the neighboring Santa Barbara Channel region, where Late Period populations were much higher and the exchange using shell-bead money more intensive. Population growth along the Santa Barbara Channel may have spilled into neighboring regions, including the Vandenberg region. Indeed, a significant increase in regional population densities occurred in many parts of California beginning about 1000 B.P. or somewhat later, and, not surprisingly, both technological and economic developments analogous to those in the Santa Barbara Channel and neighboring regions occurred elsewhere as well.

With the increasing pressure on shellfish communities that I discussed above, it is expectable that utilization of other protein sources would have been intensified during the Late Period. The increase in shore fishing is one example. Although hook-and-line continued to be one means used for acquiring fish, I have wondered whether Late Period populations also began to use beach seines, or to use them more intensively than before. The Santa Barbara Channel Chumash are reported to have used seines from boats rather than from shore (Hudson and Blackburn 1979:163–164), but in light of the minimal ethnographic and ethnohistorical information available regarding all Chumash subsistence pursuits, it is not unreasonable to propose that beach seines also were used. Seine fishing would have been difficult in the heavy surf along the Vandenberg coast, but there are times, especially during the summer when surf is not so intense, when seine fishing would be possible, particularly at locations where promontories afforded some protection from the full brunt of the surf. Seines require a good deal of effort to manufacture and maintain, but they would have vastly increased the catch for the amount of time spent fishing. Because the array of fish taxa and their proportional abundances should be relatively distinctive if seines were used, the possibility of their use during the Late Period could be addressed through taxonomic identification of larger collections of fish bone from Vandenberg sites than are currently available.

The intensive harvesting of freshwater birds at the mouth of the Santa Ynez River is more evidence of expansion of subsistence activities during the Late Period. It is possible that large numbers of birds were acquired through the use of nets. Ethnographic or ethnohistorical descriptions of the use of nets for catching freshwater birds elsewhere in California and in the Great Basin provide some idea of how this may have been done. The nets have the approximate shape and size of a volleyball net, and they are stretched between poles across an area of water where resting birds might fly if spooked from the proper direction. As well, there is ethnographic evidence that the Santa Barbara Channel Chumash used duck corrals, which were enclosures made of bulrush reeds with zig-zag entrances through which ducks might be herded (Hudson and Blackburn 1979:63). Casting nets also might have been used, but, if so, one would expect to find in Late Period sites the weights attached to the particularly in the selection of appropriate samples of shell or charcoal, so that both the quantity and quality of chronological information is being enhanced. By the end of the twentieth century the number of dated sites will have at least doubled, and we will be in a much better position to discern fluctuations in regional population density.

Tighter control over the chronology of occupation at individual sites will allow finer chronological divisions to be used in monitoring change in diet and subsistence technology. Such control is important because the chronology of environmental fluctuations I developed contains more divisions than the four-part archaeological chronology I used. As a consequence, I was not able to determine whether some of the environmental fluctuations were accompanied by concomitant changes in diet or subsistence technology. Indeed, the relationships I proposed between environmental change on the one hand and diet and subsistence technology on the other should be treated as hypotheses having tentative support from available data. Although identifying the nature of these relationships is difficult and will require substantially more data to clarify than were available to me, knowledge of how these variables relate to each other is fundamental to our understanding of the Vandenberg region's prehistory.

The most challenging objective of future research in the Vandenberg region is to understand why it was that earlier in prehistory human population density responded more closely to environmental fluctuations than was the case later in prehistory. I have proposed some tentative answers to this question, and I believe my proposals are viable avenues of future investigation. The answers, whatever they turn out to be, will require further development of cultural evolutionary theory, which means that archaeology of the Vandenberg region has a chance to contribute in a very fundamental way to our understanding of cultural development of hunter-gatherers.

8

Retrospects and Prospects

INTRODUCTION

Having worked many late nights and weekends to finish the technical report on my Vandenberg research for the National Park Service, I felt mentally exhausted when it finally was completed and wondered whether the knowledge contained in the report was really worth the several years I devoted to the Shuttle Project. Not having contract obligations weighing on my mind during the ensuing years, I eventually arrived at a more dispassionate viewpoint. I realized that, despite the many hassles of administering a relatively large project and the duress of completing data analysis and report preparation with only wisps of funds left in the budget, I had become a much wiser archaeologist through acquisition of new insights into the prehistory of coastal California and the theory of hunter-gatherer adaptations. Now it was my challenge to build upon the findings of the technical report and to share my insights with my colleagues and the public interested in archaeology and the prehistory of California. The study I have presented in the preceding pages is one step in reaching this goal.

In these final pages I wish to reflect on several topics to which I have given only slight attention up to this point but that deserve a few more words. In particular, I want to give attention to some of the benefits of marine food resources to prehistoric coast-dwellers and to the current status of archaeological resources on Vandenberg Air Force Base.

THE ATTRACTION OF MARINE FOOD RESOURCES

Osborn was essentially correct in arguing in his 1977 article that shellfish and other marine foods generally rank lower than terrestrial mammals from the perspective of optimal foraging theory. What he failed to recognize, however, is that people living near a coast with a bountiful marine environment readily include marine resources in the breadth of their diet because of periodic unavailability of terrestrial mammals. In other words, marine resources will not be ranked so low that they would never be considered until terrestrial mammals become scarce relative to the population size of human predators. I do not believe that large terrestrial mammals such as deer ever were so regularly available in the Vandenberg region, or in most other regions along the Pacific coast, that hunter-gatherers were able to sate themselves on venison or the meat of other game animals every day of the year.

In all fairness to Alan Osborn, other archaeologists also have downplayed the role of shellfish relative to other resources (see, for instance, Cohen 1977:79). Moreover, I am not the only archaeologist studying prehistoric shellfish-eaters who has emphasized the important role that shellfish may have played. My colleagues Jon Erlandson and Terry Jones, both of whom also work in coastal California, have argued eloquently that collection of shellfish has many important advantages over acquisition of other animal foods (Erlandson 1988; Jones 1991:435). Farther afield, Jeffrey Quilter and Terry Stocker (1983) have pointed out the considerably greater food value available from mussels than estimated by Osborn, and they propose that shellfish and other sea foods played an important role in the emergence of cultural complexity among preceramic peoples along the Peruvian coast.

When deer and other game animals were not readily acquired, mussels were always available to Vandenberg hunter-gatherers. Mussels were a highly reliable food resource because they are very abundant in rocky intertidal zones and grow to an edible size within a few years. Furthermore, Vandenberg residents always knew the locations of mussel beds because mussels do not move, and they could be collected with bare hands or at most a stick to pry them loose. Some sort of container such as a basket for carrying the mussels back to camp was the only other item of technology needed. In contrast, deer hunting entails the use of a projectile and a device for propelling the projectile (atlatl and dart or bow and arrow)—technological items requiring a good deal of time and effort to manufacture and skill to use effectively. While projectiles could be reused many times, several generally would be needed for a hunt, and they had to be replaced or repaired from time to time due to breakage, damage, or loss.

Even though seals and sea lions generally are very wary and quite difficult to hunt in an aquatic setting, at times they require very little hunting effort. Seals occasionally come ashore onto a sandy beach, and both seals and sea lions will haul out on bedrock shelves exposed at low tide. In certain ideal locations, a hunter might stalk the hauled-out animals and come close enough with relative ease to make a kill using either a harpoon or club. While pinnipeds seldom unwittingly exposed themselves to easy predation, the vicarious hunter probably would continually monitor the locations where an easy kill was occasionally possible. In general, deer hunting probably was more reliable so long as deer were relatively abundant, but a hunter undoubtedly always took advantage of the occasional opportunity to make an easy kill of a seal or sea lion.

In short, knowing the average rate of return of the highest-ranked food resources does not necessarily allow us to understand why marine foods such as shellfish and sea mammals were exploited. The rates of return of high-ranked food resources such as deer fluctuated from day to day, season to season, and year to year, and there were times when consistently available marine foods, although low-ranked on the average, were needed to compensate for shortfalls. By the end of the Late Period, shortfalls in the availability of deer had become permanent in the Vandenberg region. Based on studies of modern mule deer populations living on the base, hunting this animal could provide 2,789 kg of protein per year without endangering the viability of the deer population. However, the annual protein requirement of the approximately 300

Purisimeño Chumash would have been on the order of 5,475 kg (Glassow and Wilcoxon 1988:42). Consequently, deer could provide only about half of the protein required by the Chumash living in the region at the time of European contact. This is surely one of the reasons why greater emphasis was placed on fish and freshwater birds during the Late Period.

THE NEGLECTED REALMS OF CULTURE: SOCIAL ORGANIZATION AND IDEOLOGY

There are two reasons why the focus of my research has been on subsistence change rather than on two other major aspects of culture: social organization and ideology. First, most archaeological data from sites occupied by hunter-gatherers concerns subsistence, including diet and technology involved in acquiring and processing foods. The best sources of information on social organization, and to some extent ideology, are stylistic characteristics of artifacts, artifact associations with architecture, and mortuary remains in cemeteries. Vandenberg sites do not contain an abundance of artifacts having rich stylistic content; architecture is poorly preserved in Vandenberg sites, and at any rate would require extensive and costly excavations to expose; and cemetery excavations not only are illegal according to California law but are of great concern to Native American groups. The second reason for my research focus is that knowledge of subsistence systems is an excellent starting point for investigating the other aspects of culture. Much of hunter-gatherer social organization, but certainly not all of it, is dependent on the nature of subsistence systems. In addition, many aspects of social organization are dependent on settlement systems, but these are largely dependent on subsistence systems as well. It makes sense, consequently, to understand both subsistence and settlement systems before tackling the more difficult problem of explicating the nature of hunter-gatherer social organization and ideology. I do not mean to say that social organization and ideology cannot be studied in the absence of much knowledge of subsistence and settlement systems; they certainly can. However, the task would be much easier and more rewarding with prior knowledge of subsistence and settlement.

There are good reasons why social organization should never be completely disregarded while focusing one's attention on subsistence, particularly if settlement systems also are of interest. I mentioned in Chapter 7 that the anomalous absence of projectile points and biface manufacturing waste products in the Initial Early Period deposits of SBA-552 may have been the result of males spending much, or even most, of their time away from this residential base. Regardless of whether this particular hypothesis is borne out by future research, it does highlight the potential importance of gender in accounting for archaeological variability at the level of settlement systems. Archaeologists frequently have proposed that certain sites were occupied only by males on a hunting trek, and ethnographic examples of such camps abound. But little consideration has been given to the possibility that a residential base may have been nearly the exclusive domain of women and children in some prehistoric settlement systems.

Until recently, in fact, archaeologists have given very little attention to the possibility of identifying gender roles in the archaeological record and to the likelihood that these roles changed significantly over the course of time. More fundamentally, as Margaret Conkey and Janet Spector (1984) have pointed out, archaeology and ethnology have been biased toward a male's view of cultural systems and frequently have neglected or minimized women's activities and social status. In the archaeology of hunter-gatherers, for instance, a good deal of attention has been devoted to the manufacture and use of projectile points—typically male-related artifacts—but little attention has been given to milling implements, typically female-related artifacts.

This situation is beginning to change, and although the roots of gender studies in archaeology may be traced back to feminist anthropology of the 1970s, both male and female archaeologists are now contributing interesting studies of gender. In California, for instance, Tom Jackson (1991) studied the relationship between women's activities and bedrock mortar sites in the Sierra Nevada. These bedrock mortars came into use about 1,000 years ago, and they reflect the importance of acorns as a food staple, much as "portable" mortars do beginning much earlier in coastal southern California. Jackson argues that settlement systems changed at this time as a result of the importance of bedrock mortar sites and the areas of land surrounding them from which acorns were collected. Therefore, it was women's activities, and the food-processing facilities they owned or at least managed, that determined where sites were located. With regard to cultural change occurring about 1,000 years ago in the Sierra Nevada, women clearly played a key role. During the Initial Early Period in the Vandenberg region, women's subsistence activities may have similarly influenced settlement patterns.

Regarding other aspects of social organization, I have discussed in different contexts studies by Chester King and Jeanne Arnold, both of whom have been interested in the evolution of sociopolitical complexity in the Santa Barbara Channel region. King has been concerned with the social and political correlates of shell beads and ornaments associated with the dead in prehistoric cemeteries, while Arnold has looked at the context of craft specialization and control of intervillage exchange in the evolution of political complexity. Their contributions reflect a growing interest in the emergence of social complexity among hunter-gatherers in many parts of the world. Some ten years ago Douglas Price and James Brown (1985) summarized much of the thinking about the nature and origins of hunter-gatherer social complexity in their introduction to a volume of articles on this subject. More recently, Herbert Maschner and Brian Fagan (1991) brought together a series of articles concerning complexity of hunter-gatherer societies along the north Pacific coast. These two sets of articles, as well as other discussions of hunter-gather social complexity in the archaeological literature, give testimony to the potential to address the subject of social complexity with archaeological data. At the same time, however, they demonstrate the difficulties in defining more than the grossest aspects of social complexity.

In Chapter 2, for instance, I mentioned that the Purisimeño Chumash who lived north of Point Conception probably were not socially as complex as the Chumash who lived along the Santa Barbara Channel. Ethnohistoric data hints at this distinction, which is expectable in light of the absence of plank canoes north of Point Conception and the intensive cross-channel trade that accompanied canoe use. However,

I am unable to point to specific aspects of the archaeological record that reflect this difference in social organization. Surely there are differences in the archaeological records of the two regions indicative of variations in social complexity, but a research program focused on this problem would have to be devised in order to generate the appropriate data.

I can say much less about the subject of ideology, that is, about religious ritual, moral systems, cosmology, symbolism reflecting social differences, and the like. The only artifacts I collected in the course of the Shuttle Project possibly related to ideology are shell beads, small nodules of red ocher, "charmstones," small shale tablets with incised geometric designs, and shaped stone objects that may be effigies. Artifacts in all these categories are rare in the project collections, and their specific ideological contexts are unknown.

Perhaps the most spectacular aspect of the archaeological record pertaining to Chumash ideology is rock art, which takes the form of pictographs painted on the rock walls of overhangs and rock shelters. The Chumash produced some of the most elaborate pictographic rock art in the world, although there is considerable variation between bizarre motifs of abstract zoomorphic figures carefully executed in several colors and simple geometric designs in red ocher. Curiously, the ethnohistoric and ethnographic records are essentially silent on the subject. Nonetheless, at least the more elaborate rock art undoubtedly was related to ritual activity, and many of the symbols, which are repeated from one locality to another, must have had specific meanings to the Chumash. Beginning with the efforts of Campbell Grant (1965), there has been a series of painstaking efforts to accurately document Chumash rock art through photography and drawing, which is critically necessary given that it is gradually disappearing as a result of natural erosion and purposeful or inadvertent defacement. The several rock art sites on Vandenberg recently have undergone careful documentation as part of a larger effort to inventory the base's cultural resources.

As might be imagined, both archaeologists and amateur rock art enthusiasts have speculated on the meaning and ritual context of the rock art. For instance, symbols consisting of concentric circles and sawtooth rays are believed by some to be solstice motifs, and certain caves containing these symbols are suspected to be solstice shrines (Hudson and Underhay 1978). Some archaeologists, however, have attempted to understand the cultural context of Chumash rock art by looking at such characteristics as geographic context, complexity of the panels, and association with habitation sites. William Hyder (1989), for instance, was able to demonstrate that some Chumash rock art sites undoubtedly were associated with ceremonial activities, whereas other rock art sites had more secular contexts. Even though he was not able to relate particular motifs or combinations of motifs with specific meanings or activities, he began the task of developing testable hypotheses regarding the varying social and ideological contexts of Chumash rock art.

HINDSIGHT IS ALWAYS 20-20

After completing a long and complex piece of research, an archaeologist inevitably asks two related questions of him- or herself: "What would I have done differently if

I could do the project over again, and what improvements might I make in undertaking similar projects in the future? My immediate answer to both questions was to be very cautious about committing myself to such a project in the future, and indeed I may never again decide to direct a project as large and complex as the Shuttle Project. Even if I do not, other archaeologists might benefit from my hindsight view of the Shuttle Project.

Any archaeological project, no matter how large or small, must be planned around a variety of constraints, including available funds and various impositions such as accessibility of sites for investigation. This is especially the case with projects undertaken to meet specific cultural resource management needs. For example, the 1974 phase of work on South Vandenberg had to involve sites that might be affected by construction of space shuttle facilities and had to be a wide-ranging testing program in order to obtain information relevant to evaluating the significance of sites in terms of criteria for inclusion on the National Register of Historic Places. In a cultural resource management context, the objective is to design the project so that it accomplishes management goals as efficiently and effectively as possible while at the same time maximizing the generation of information relevant to regional prehistory.

The 1974 testing program relied on one to several test units excavated at each of 31 archaeological sites. The problem with test units is that they entail investing all the effort that can be expended at a site into obtaining a sample from just a few locations. Given the management goals of the 1974 program, I suspect that more useful information probably could have been generated from a series of solid cores about 10 cm to 15 cm in diameter taken from ten or more locations across the area of each site. Most of the 31 sites are accessible by a truck equipped with a coring rig, and the cores obtained could have been treated like column samples because the soils in them would have been intact. The less accessible sites could have been tested using a hand-operated bucket auger, which yields less-than-ideal samples because the soils are churned by the auger. However, such samples still would have been quite useful. The coring could have been accomplished with a relatively small crew over a period of a few weeks, thus saving considerable funds in field crew wages that could then be devoted to more intensive laboratory processing of the core and auger samples and a more comprehensive radiocarbon dating program.

Such a data collection strategy would have provided a good deal of information on the stratification of midden deposits and the areal variations in midden constituents. As well, the amounts of faunal remains would have been adequate for characterizing the variations in major faunal categories such as those used in my analysis. A coring program nonetheless has its disadvantages. Ten to 20 cores per site would not result in very large samples of artifacts, and the information on stratification of deposits would be minimal. At most sites, however, artifact collections from a few units would be very small, and stratification is usually ambiguous; only at SBA-210 and 552 would using cores as opposed to units make a big difference in the number of artifacts recovered. In terms of the goals of the 1974 testing program, these sorts of sacrifices certainly would have been tolerable. With respect to the goals of the study presented in the previous chapters, I believe the quality of data from a coring program would have been much higher.

.

The strategy of collecting less and analyzing more intensively also may be applied to rethinking the data recovery program of 1978–80. I believe I would have had sufficient data for my analysis had I halved the size of the units screened through eighth-inch mesh, although I would have sorted the residues caught by the screens into the same relatively specific constituent categories. With the laboratory time and effort saved, I would have been able to undertake a more comprehensive analysis of faunal remains and probably would have learned a lot more about dietary variability.

Instead of using quarter-inch mesh screens for sifting deposits from all of the remaining units, I would have opted for half-inch mesh screening for the majority, if not all. This would have freed up time and effort for excavation of a larger areal exposure in Area A of SBA-931 and an intensive analysis of artifact distributions within this exposure. As well, the approach would have increased the sample size of larger artifacts, including among others typeable projectile point fragments, other flaked stone tools, ground stone implements, and tarring pebbles. Such artifacts typically are in low densities in California sites, so large volumes of deposits must be excavated in order to obtain samples of reasonable size.

In recent years, many archaeologists working in California have sacrificed the objective of obtaining a collection of larger artifacts sufficient for intersite comparative analysis in favor of collecting adequate samples of very small items caught by eighth-inch or even sixteenth-inch screens. In part, the emphasis during the last two decades on fine-mesh screening and sorting in a laboratory of all residues caught by screens was a reaction to the earlier unsystematic recovery of small artifacts and faunal remains that inevitably results from use of quarter-inch screens and sorting during excavation while the unwashed residues remain in the screen. At the same time, archaeologists became more interested in obtaining systematic samples of faunal remains of all sizes in order to undertake dietary analyses of the type presented in the last chapter. Many California archaeologists still have not come to grips with the problem of how to obtain adequate samples of both relatively small and relatively large cultural items in coastal California sites. From the perspective of hindsight, I could have undertaken the coarser form of data recovery I used at SBA-539 at all the impact areas once adequate fine-screened samples had been collected.

The key to solving this problem, of course, is to use a variety of screen mesh sizes and to partition the total volume excavated between the mesh sizes in such a way that samples of all classes of artifacts and faunal remains are adequate for analytical purposes. Nonetheless, such a strategy is relevant only if there is the potential to excavate a relatively large volume of deposits. In many instances this is not the case. If I could excavate no more than a few cubic meters from a site, or if time and effort resources were very limited, I would opt for using exclusively fine-mesh screens and emphasizing analysis of faunal remains, which generally are abundant enough in coastal California sites that small volumes can yield adequate samples. The fact is, however, that California archaeologists often do have the chance to excavate relatively large volumes of deposits, and they could optimize the data collected by using a greater variety of mesh sizes in screening deposits.

A caveat should be added to this perspective. Because an archaeological excavation inevitably destroys site deposits, archaeologists generally attempt to excavate as little as possible to address research problems. In this way we are able to conserve archaeological resources and use them wisely. Indeed, many archaeologists feel that research problems requiring large volumes of excavation should be given low priority until we have exhausted the prospects of addressing research problems requiring small volumes. Because research problems concerning subsistence may be addressed through relatively small excavation volumes, this conservation ethic lies behind much of the emphasis on subsistence studies in coastal California archeology over the last few decades. Certainly the conservation ethic always should be acknowledged in designing a research project, but there are situations in which large-volume excavation is justified and indeed should be undertaken. Specifically, there are instances in which sites will be entirely or partially destroyed once archaeological investigations have been completed. The appropriate ethic in these circumstances is to maximize the information obtained from a site given constraints of funding and time.

The final change I would institute if I were to undertake new research at Vandenberg sites would be to be more selective of the samples selected for radiocarbon dating, and I would attempt to devote more project funds to obtaining radiocarbon dates. The ideal sample from a seemingly homogeneous midden, one that no doubt has been extensively churned by rodent burrowing, is a single piece of shell or a dense clump of charcoal chunks. In many cases the size of the sample may be smaller than the 30 g–100 g of shell or 10 g–20 g of charcoal ideal for radiocarbon dating. However, frequently a shell or chunk of charcoal is large enough if the radiocarbon laboratory counts the C-14 emissions a longer length of time than normal. This procedure costs more money, but the resulting utility of the radiocarbon date would be worth the additional cost. Some of the radiocarbon dates obtained from Vandenberg sites since the late 1980s are based on samples as small as 0.01 g of carbon. A procedure known as accelerator mass spectrometry (AMS) is used to obtain radiocarbon dates on such small samples. Unfortunately the cost of an AMS date is twice to three times that of a conventional date, making it impractical for larger-scale dating programs.

THE CONTRIBUTIONS OF ARCHAEOLOGICAL RESEARCH PERFORMED UNDER CONTRACT

During the last 20 years the vast majority of funds for archaeological research in the United States have come from contracts with governmental agencies or from land-developing firms complying with governmental regulations. Furthermore, most archaeologists directing this research are not connected with academic institutions; instead they either head their own contracting firms or are employed by companies involved with environmental assessment and development planning. Another large cadre of archaeologists directing research projects works for federal or state agencies concerned with land management. All this means that our knowledge of regional prehistories throughout the United States is increasing at an unprecedented rate, and this increase in knowledge no longer is dominated by the contributions of archaeologists in academic positions at universities or in curatorial positions at museums.